BORN ASTRIDE THE GRAVE

One woman's reflections on mortality

To Janet

With love & warmest wishes

Gill

Gill Spendlove

Grosvenor House
Publishing Limited

This book is published by
Grosvenor House Publishing Ltd
Link House
140 The Broadway, Tolworth, Surrey, KT6 7HT.
www.grosvenorhousepublishing.co.uk

A CIP record for this book
is available from the British Library

ISBN 978-1-83975-319-0

There would be no chance at all of getting to know death if it happened only once. But fortunately life is nothing but a continuing dance of birth and death, a dance of change. Every time I hear the rush of a mountain stream, or the waves crashing on the shore, or my own heartbeat, I hear the sound of impermanence. These changes, these small deaths, are our living links with death. They are death's pulses, death's heartbeat, prompting us to let go of all the things we cling to.

Sogyal Rinpoche: "The Tibetan Book of Living and Dying"

Death is not anything......death is not.......It's the absence of presence, nothing more..................the endless time of never coming back..........................a gap you can't see, and when the wind blows through it, it makes no sound.

Tom Stoppard: "Rosencrantz and Guildenstern are Dead"

Contents

Front cover: *"Fallen Leaves"* by John Denaro

Grave Beginnings

Since the day of my birth, my death began its walk.
It is walking toward me without hurrying.
Jean Cocteau

I'm not sure at what point I first became aware of the concept of death but I remember waking up one morning as a very small child convinced that I had died.

I slept in a room on my own and on that particular morning I had woken up completely unable to open my eyes. I tried a variety of techniques to rectify the problem starting with a long, slow concerted effort to prise the eyelids apart by the sheer force of will and concluding with an attempt to sneak up and catch them unawares with a sudden burst of energy in order to break through the vice-like grip of whatever was holding them but, try as I might, I could not get the eyelids to separate in the manner I was used to and, after battling unsuccessfully for some time, I reached the only possible conclusion which was that I must be dead.

As this realisation slowly dawned, I felt the first stirrings of fear. My heart seemed to beat more loudly in my chest as I began to wonder what this new and unexplored state would mean for me. Clearly it rendered me unable to see but what other restrictions might it impose I wondered and were there any advantages? Where was I exactly? Was I still in my small bedroom in Chaddesden or had I been spirited away somehow to some other-worldly place, isolated for ever from friends and family and from everything familiar?

And what ought I to do? Ought I to lie wherever I was and simply wait for something to happen or should I initiate some activity and if so, what? What does one do when one is dead? I remember feeling somewhat put out that I had received no instruction in this matter. I had been instructed in all sorts of matters such as how to hold a knife and fork and not to speak when my mouth was full; how to excuse myself from the meal table and when to say please and thankyou: how to put my clothes on properly, use a handkerchief and tie my shoelaces. The list, in fact, seemed endless but there had been nothing to tell me what I should do if I should discover that I had died. I was on my own with this one and indecision rendered me motionless; trapped in limbo between all that I had learnt and the unknown.

It was at this point that I heard the familiar sound of the bedroom door quietly opening and my mother's voice saying, "Come on, up you get. It's a lovely day. The sun is shining". Relief flooded through me. I could still hear and what's more it seemed that Mum was in this strange place with me. Things were not so bad after all. But she was behaving as if everything was the same as usual. Perhaps she didn't realise that we had died.

Anxious and confused, I struggled to sit upright and to explain my predicament. "I can't see. I can't open my eyes. I think I must have died," I blurted out in a garbled rush. I caught the hint of a smile in her voice as she assured me that I was very much alive and all that was needed to restore normality was a little water which was fetched immediately and used to bathe back my sight. How quick was my return from the dead! The experience, however, was vivid and profound and has remained with me through the years.

Another strange thing that marked my childhood was the frequent occurrence of what I described as "funny feelings". An unsettling feeling would descend on me, starting in my stomach and slowly working its way round the rest of my body, gradually increasing in intensity and concluding inside my head. The feeling had elements of anxiety and disorientation which gradually gave way to what I can only describe as otherworldliness; a feeling of wonder, of heightened reality and a sense of something beyond the present moment and beyond our knowing. These feelings might descend at any time and in any place and all I could do was wait for them to pass.

There was something vaguely frightening about inhabiting this strange landscape and if my mother was near, I would slip my hand in hers and quietly say, "I have a funny feeling mummy". Inevitably she would ask what sort of feeling and I was never able to tell her.

In later life I have often pondered on the meaning of those episodes. They seem to indicate an awareness of some kind of existence beyond our present reality. Maybe I was trailing Wordsworth's "clouds of glory". I doubt I will ever really know. I no longer have them. They gradually became less frequent until they disappeared altogether but they had a lasting effect on me which I think contributed to the fascination with death that I had from a very young age: a fascination made evident each year on our annual holiday.

I was the youngest of three children, the only girl, so I was often at odds with my siblings. On family holidays we took it in turn to choose the morning activity and invariably my choice was to visit the grave of Anne Bronte much to the frustration of my brothers who would just as predictably groan and complain with objections such as, "Again! We've already done that..... loads of times........it's borin'". But it wasn't "borin'" to me and so the whole family would trudge its way through the streets of the seaside town of Scarborough to the requested graveside.

I'm not sure exactly what it was that pulled me there with such force, something to do with the quiet solemnity of the place, the uncompromising presence of the solid headstone whose words still are etched on my mind just as surely as they were on the stone: "Here lie the remains of Anne Brontë, Daughter of the Reverend P. Brontë".

I had a feeling that I was in the presence of something special, something mysterious and something that would somehow cast its shadow across the rest of my life. I could not have explained it that way as that young child but I definitely had a sense of it.

Even so my parents strove to shield me from the harsh realities of death in the belief that this was in my interest and so as a child I remember a maiden aunt hidden behind a closed door through which the grown-ups would disappear from time to time. There seemed to be a lot of whispering and secrets and Aunt Flo was always referred to in hushed tones. Years later I discovered that she was dying of terminal cancer but this information belonged to the grown up world, a world from which I was most definitely excluded.

I remember going home from school for lunch one day and being met by our next-door neighbour who we affectionately referred to as Mrs J. She told me my Mum had been called away. Something in the manner of Mrs J conveyed the gravity of what had happened. I knew that whatever it was, was so serious that it meant my Mum was unable to be at home to give me lunch. She had never before been absent.

The interruption of my daily routine cast me adrift and left me floundering for something to hold on to, some explanation and understanding of the situation that was unfolding. "Aunt Flo has gone to Jesus," I was informed, and I struggled to imagine what that could possibly mean. I felt the heavy weight of unexplained sadness choking back any words I may have had so that my unease and confusion remained unspoken. I guess the grown-ups were trying to shield me from something they felt was beyond my years to comprehend but the vaguely furtive nature of their behaviour had left me with little understanding of what had taken place and its possible consequences. I had no idea what I should be feeling or how I should behave. This was new territory, fascinating and frightening in equal measure.

I didn't attend Aunt Flo's funeral. In fact, as a child I never attended any funerals. Various distant relatives died and Mum and Dad would put on their best clothes and disappear for a few hours returning with news of who they'd seen and a vague comment on the service. Funerals it seems were grown up occasions and had nothing really to do with me.

But, in spite of my parents' best efforts to airbrush the spectre of death from my everyday reality, it continued to prowl along the edges of my childhood. Apparently, it was impossible to exclude as one perfectly ordinary evening in 1963, I was sitting under our dining room table. A red tablecloth hung low over its edges making it feel safe and den-like and providing a retreat from the general chatter and noise of family life going on around me.

Everything was fairly relaxed because it was a Friday evening, the beginning of the weekend. I was dimly aware that the television was on but it was of no interest to me as I was engrossed in my own little world. Suddenly I became aware of a significant change in the atmosphere as Dad demanded quiet from everyone and Mum repeated the word, "Newsflash". There was an urgency in the way they both spoke that alerted me to the fact that something very serious was happening: grown up stuff no doubt which I did not understand but which nevertheless filled me with a sense of dread. My hideaway no longer felt quite so safe as I strained to make sense of what my parents were saying.

I think I picked up that the President of the United States had been shot dead but I couldn't really understand the significance of this for us. America was a very long way away wasn't it? Nevertheless, I didn't doubt that something cataclysmic had taken place and my sense of this was visceral. Death had once again left its mark on me so powerfully that over 50 years later I still recall the chill that shrouded me that November evening.

Some years later was another such intrusion. I was at junior school but usually went home at dinnertime where Mum would be waiting for me with a hot meal, a warm welcome and the enquiry, "What have you been up to this morning?"

This particular day I returned home to a hot meal as usual but nothing else felt quite the same. I noticed the drone of the television coming from the corner of the dining room which was very unusual for this time of day and then I noticed that there were tears running down my Mum's face. I had never seen Mum cry before and I found the sight strangely frightening. Tentatively I asked her why she was crying and she just said simply, "I was just thinking how it would be if it was you."

At first, I could make no sense of this but gradually the flickering black and white television images revealed the tragedy unfolding of a junior school in a Welsh mining valley consumed by tons of waste from the local colliery. The school had been full of children and rescue workers were wading through the debris in an effort to save lives.

It was an oddly quiet dinnertime with Mum hardly speaking. The familiar question, "What have you been doing this morning?" never came and that afternoon I returned to school with a vague and ill-defined sense of the power of death. Events in what was to me then a far away village were impacting on us here and it registered in my body as a strong sense of unease.

It struck me as shocking that children the same age as me could just die like that. That a day could begin with everything just as normal and within minutes turn into a nightmare of death and devastation.

Many years later I thought back to that tragedy of October 1966 in Aberfan and was hit anew by the enormity of it. By then I was a teacher and one of my young pupils, aged twelve, had been killed in a road accident. He was knocked down on his way to school running to catch the school bus. For the rest of the year there was an empty space where he had sat except it wasn't empty. Every time I looked at it I saw his absence. He had been a joy to have in the classroom. He was kind to his peers, enthusiastic about most things and full of the joy of life. He was poised on the brink of adolescence and had so much to give and to explore. This potential had been snatched away and it was heart breaking in a way that only the death of a child can be.

All those years ago a village lost 116 of its children. That day innocence was massacred on an incomprehensible scale. Had the coal tip moved twenty minutes earlier, the school would have been empty. Had my young pupil tried to cross the road just a minute or two later or earlier he would not have been hit. Life and death turn on such narrow margins.

Death it seems could not be avoided and so surely it was only a matter of time before it fully invaded my own life. I would try to imagine the death of my parents, struggle to grasp what it might be like, wrestle with the concept of them no longer being here. How would it be? Here one minute, gone the next? A slow slide from existence to non existence? And, no matter the manner of the disappearance, the resulting void would be so unbearably desolate that something would fall away in my stomach rendering me unable to continue with the exploration of the idea. Then one weekday morning the awfulness of this reality crept a little closer.

When I was at junior school there was a little boy I called my boyfriend. His name was Stephen Booth. He was a skinny little boy with fine features and very blue, sparkling eyes. He could perhaps have been described as fragile, if not before the event I am about to relate then definitely after it.

On this particular morning I was in my classroom, seated in my place as usual at a table surrounded by familiar faces. It was just an ordinary morning, or so I thought. After the teacher had delivered her instructions, we all fell eagerly to work on the given task. It was then that events took an unexpected turn. Stephen Booth cut through our activity to state, "My Dad died last night." There was a stunned silence round the table as we all struggled to digest this information. Was he serious? Could this be true? How could this happen? Had we heard right and if so what should we now say or do?

One brave soul, groping for understanding tentatively enquired, "What do you mean?" and Stephen simply repeated his original utterance no more able to explain it than we were to understand what exactly it meant. But I noticed something in his eyes that had not been there before and, in that instant, I knew that he was forever lost to me. He had tasted of a knowledge way beyond my imagining.

If I had ever asked the question, what does a small boy look like when his father has been stolen away in the night? I now knew the answer. He looked just like Stephen did right now – lost, confused and alone: forever different to his schoolmates.

The teacher interrupted our confusion to send Stephen off round the school under the pretence of delivering a message, so that she could announce to the whole class what had befallen him. Her announcement was met with the same stunned silence that we had experienced a few minutes earlier. We were instructed to be especially kind to him. Was that it? An extra dose of kindness would fix it all for him? Somehow I doubted it but it seemed like the best advice we were likely to get. So all we friends worked especially hard to be super, super kind when he returned. Our friend, Carol, certainly went the extra mile in her version of kind, for which she paid dearly. She ripped her vocabulary book into hundreds of tiny pieces in an effort to make him laugh. It worked and she considered her lost playtime and one hundred lines a small price to pay for it.

I never saw Stephen in quite the same way after that day regarding him with a mixture of awe and fear. I think he was a reminder that it was possible for people just like us to lose a parent with no warning. Here one minute and gone the next just as I had feared. That death could strike in the midst of a perfectly ordinary day or night and having struck that nothing could ever be the same again.

We stayed friends for a while, Stephen and I, soaring high together on the playground swings, spinning crazily on the teapot lid, running, dodging and playing catch but the unbridled pleasure of childhood like sand had slipped through our grasp. From time to time, Stephen would tell me that he was the man of the house now and had to be brave for his Mum, a burden surely too great for a small boy to carry. The night Death came for Stephen's father, he took Stephen's childhood along with him.

We transferred from junior to secondary school and shortly afterwards Stephen and his Mum left the area and I never saw him again. But he left a strong impression on me and occasionally, even now, I wonder whatever became of lovely, fragile, fatherless Stephen Booth.

Pets Are People Too, You Know!

Until one has loved an animal a part of one's soul remains unawakened.
Anatole France

With the move to secondary school came new beginnings and I became friendly with a girl who lived just round the corner from me. Her name was Linda and I was slightly in awe of her mainly because she had the most exquisitely long, chestnut brown hair while I was forced by my Mum to have an excruciatingly short style, so short in fact that on more than one occasion I was mistaken for a boy, deeply unpleasant experiences. How marvellous it must be to have a mother who would allow you to grow your hair so long I reflected. This was way beyond my imagining.

But there was something else I admired about Linda and that was the fact that she had a perfect little black poodle named Sooty who would often accompany her when we played on our local park. He was smart and obedient and Linda would proudly demonstrate the tricks she had taught him: how he balanced across benches and would stay obediently in a given spot until she gave the command to move. I thought how great it would be if I could have a dog of my own to teach tricks and to keep Sooty company but I had more chance of being allowed to grow my hair long than of having a dog.

Linda, however, had a solution. An elderly couple she called The Pedleys lived on her street and they had a dog who could be the answer to my prayers. It was a small, white poodle called Kim. What could be better? And Linda was sure they would let us walk him because Mr Pedley had recently had a stroke which had rendered them both virtually housebound. In response to this situation, Kim had developed the habit of taking himself for a walk through the local streets to the park and back. This, of course, was before the days of dog wardens when unaccompanied dogs were not an uncommon sight. I realised that I had seen him on his habitual route on more than one occasion but had not realised that he was a poodle. He wasn't usually clipped in the traditional way but his fur was left to grow more naturally and I liked this about him.

Linda assured me that all we needed to do was to turn up at the Pedleys and offer to walk this dog and she was right. We turned up and, hey presto, I suddenly had a dog. Not only that but the Pedleys were extremely grateful for the offer. They didn't like him making his own way through the streets while feeling unable to stop him.

I felt so proud walking to the park with my little, white dog on his lead. But it wasn't long before dissatisfaction set in as I realised that Kim couldn't do any of the tricks that Sooty could. It seemed that it wasn't as straightforward as I had imagined. It hadn't occurred to me that dogs were not born understanding English and immediately able to do as they were told. Apparently training was required in order to achieve this and I had no idea how to go about it.

Linda was happy to let me into the secret of her training techniques which included a sharp rap with Kim's lead whenever he failed to obey a command. Many years later I discovered that this was misguided and cruel but I did not know this then.

In spite of my unkindness, Kim responded and I gradually grew to love that dog, not for any tricks he might be able to do but just for himself. He was extremely forgiving and I just loved being with him. He became woven into the pattern of my weeks and remained so long after Linda and Sooty had disappeared from the scene. Whenever I went to collect him, he would jump up high on his back legs, so excited to see me. He knew that we were off for a walk together and there was nothing he loved more.

But one day when I arrived, Kim was his usual excited self while his owner was clearly not sharing it. Mrs Pedley explained that Mr Pedley had had another stroke and he had deteriorated to the extent that she now needed to take a more hands-on role in looking after him. The problem was that Kim didn't under-stand this change of circumstances. For a while he had taken to growling every time Mrs Pedley took hold of her husband but the situation had escalated so that he was now baring his teeth and physically going for her. Kim obviously thought that he was protecting his master. He had always been more of his master's dog than his mistress's but this was clearly dangerous and unacceptable behaviour and could not be allowed to continue. I was just beginning to contemplate what was needed when Mrs Pedley said, "We think we are going to have to have him put down." I could not believe my ears – have Kim put down? Was she mad? He loved life, his walks, his master and me. It was unthinkable to have him "put down".

I quickly pointed out that he must not be "put down". I would have him. He was my pal and there was no way I was going to let anybody "put him down". I was not convinced by the euphemistic language. To me she was proposing cold blooded murder of an innocent victim. So I held on tightly to Kim's lead and we left for our walk.

I was convinced that once I had explained the situation to Mum and Dad, they would see that we had to look after Kim until the crisis was over no matter how long that was. Nothing else made any sense. And so after our walk I took Kim home with me and pleaded his case. I was shocked to receive a somewhat guarded response rather than the immediate, unreserved agreement I had expected. To me it was a no brainer, how could it not be so clear to the adults? I realised that I had a lot of work to do to secure Kim's safety but still felt I could achieve it.

I lay on the sofa and Kim lay with me as I reflected on the seriousness of the situation. This was literally a matter of life and death. Mum interrupted my thoughts as she called me for lunch and I declined the invitation explaining that I wasn't hungry.

She was not prepared to accept this and came to pull me up. I think it was at this point that Kim's fate was sealed. Just as he misinterpreted Mrs Pedley's handling of his master so he misinterpreted Mum's handling of me and, thinking he was protecting me, he went for her. She rushed from the room, closing the door on him and saying, "I see what Mrs Pedley means. We can't have that." Kim really had not helped his case but I was determined to keep him nevertheless.

That evening I returned Kim to his owners and explained that we would have him if they really couldn't cope with him. I didn't mention what had happened that afternoon but stressed that if there were further problems they should contact me and I would go and get him. They agreed and as I made my way home I was sure that I had done enough to secure Kim's safety, for now at least. However, I was twelve years old or thereabouts and I hadn't bargained for the duplicity of adults.

So it was that a few days later when I announced I was going to collect Kim for his walk, Mum looked uncomfortable and announced that she thought he had gone.

"Gone? Gone where?" I demanded.

"I think they've had to put him to sleep," she said gently.

"Put him down", "put him to sleep" - fine words to mask the harsh reality. Had Kim been murdered, cut off in his prime, silenced and stilled forever? I could not believe that this was true. Surely they could not have been so mean – to me but much worse to Kim.

Refusing to believe it, I grabbed my coat and, before anyone could stop me, I bolted round to the Pedleys to find out for myself what had happened. But as soon as I knocked on the door, my heart sank. There was no joyous barking, no mad antics of an exuberant Kim. It was ghostly quiet apart from the shuffling of Mrs Pedley as she made her way to the door. "Kim's gone," she said. "He's gone."

I noticed that even his lead had disappeared from the hook behind the door. They had got rid of every sign of him as if he had never existed – my beautiful, forgiving pal. Would he forgive them for this I wondered? I wasn't sure that I would. They had annihilated him for protecting his owner. His loyalty had signed his death warrant.

I felt incandescent with rage and frustration. Why had nobody listened to me? Why had I been so completely disregarded? I hadn't even been given the chance to say goodbye. I had let Kim down and I was devastated – way way beyond sad.

I continued to visit the Pedleys to see how they were and to run errands for them. A short while after Kim's death, Mrs Pedley came to the door with a very small poodle in her arms and I felt a white hot surge of anger at this imposter who had stolen the place that rightfully belonged to Kim.

Some time later I was haunted by the question of whether Kim's death was my fault. Had my dubious training technique created his aggression? Could

I have done more to deliver him from his fate? I will never know the answer to these questions but I carry the guilt of them even to this day.

Looking back as an adult I have some understanding of why people did what they did but I still carry with me the outrage and frustration of my childhood self and its voice cries far louder than the adult voice of hard, cold reason.

But Kim wasn't the only animal I lost in my childhood. For as long as I could remember, my Mum had had a dislike of cats. In fact so extreme was this dislike that it could more accurately be called a phobia. As a child I was completely unable to comprehend this and yet the condition must be fairly common as I have since discovered that it has multiple names – ailurophobia, felinophobia, elurophobia and just plain ordinary cat phobia. However it was labelled, I understood enough to know that it meant the chances of us ever having a pet cat were even less than being allowed to grow my hair long or have a dog.

Until one Summer's evening that is when our neighbours discovered, carelessly pushed into the hedge at the bottom of their garden, a box containing two kittens which had obviously been abandoned to their fate. They were tiny, too tiny really to have been separated from their mother and small enough to sit in the palm of my hand. What on earth was going to happen to these tiny creatures? Surely we couldn't turn them away to fend for themselves. They would never survive. And so my brothers and I began what seemed like the insurmountable task of persuading our parents to keep at least one of the kittens.

First we approached Dad, thinking that if we could get him on side then persuading Mum would be a whole lot easier. But he was resolute that the decision had to be Mum's. If she felt unable to live alongside a kitten, then it was a non starter. But we had glimpsed a slight chink in the wall of opposition as we approached Mum with the claim that it was fine with Dad if it was okay with her. Okay, so it was a slight misrepresentation of the truth but it allowed us to frame her as the cold hearted villain if she should refuse to shelter this tiny defenceless creature. We could see her weakening as we continued to harangue her with graphic descriptions of what might happen to this little kitten if we did not supply the shelter it so desperately needed.

The fact that the neighbours decided that they would keep one of the kittens seemed to clinch the deal and finally Mum gave way agreeing to a trial period. A whole list of conditions was attached to this trial and it seemed that we were being tasked with complete obedience for the rest of our days, a promise that we were more than happy to make at the time. In fact so desperate were we that we even thought we might be able to actually fulfil our promise. Against the odds it seems, victory was ours and in recognition of this we named our kitten Sammy.

At first Mum refused to be left alone with Sammy which I found unfathomable; she was so tiny and harmless. But very gradually she won even Mum's heart and we became her permanent home.

Sadly her sibling did not survive but Sammy grew to be a spirited cat with a slightly wild streak which we attributed to her difficult start in life. Occasionally she would disappear for a while returning dishevelled and sometimes filthy as if she'd been locked in a coal cellar. However, she was never gone for more than a couple of days.

Until one day she didn't reappear and each passing day we became more and more anxious until we decided to place an advertisement in our local paper asking anybody who might have seen our cat to contact us. Whenever the phone rang, we would race to answer it ever hopeful that there would be news of Sam. Finally there was...... sort of. Mum took the call but she didn't seem very hopeful. She didn't think the description sounded much like Sammy and so, although she had taken the street name of the caller, she hadn't taken the house number.

Dad and I felt it was worth following up. You never knew. There was a chance it could be Sammy and I was definitely of a mind to grasp at any chance no matter how slim. It didn't matter that we hadn't got the caller's house number, we would knock on every door in the street until we found it.

So off we went in search of our missing family member. I was secretly very hopeful in spite of the evidence to the contrary and so I felt fairly upbeat as we started our house calls. But very gradually my optimism began to ebb slowly away with each negative response and it began to dawn on us that this was an extremely long road. It literally stretched for miles and it seemed an impossible task to knock on every door.

We never did locate the original caller but we did find someone who seemed to have seen the same apparently stray cat. We left our details and with a promise that this person would contact us if this cat reappeared.

With heavy hearts we began to retrace our steps home, confident that we had done all that we could and nursing a small hope that we would eventually get to see this cat which might, just possibly might, be Sammy.

Some days later we did get this chance but it wasn't our cat and Sammy never did reappear. We never knew what had happened to her and I filled the huge void where an explanation should be with numerous scenarios of my own – some hopeful, some disturbing but none in any way satisfactory. It took a very long time to accept that our feisty, hard won feline was never coming home and even longer to let go of the scenarios that haunted both my days and nights.

Animals make their way into our hearts just as surely as do people and I missed her terribly for ages, plagued by the uncertainty of her fate. It was another very raw experience of loss and death.

Our next cat, George, met a much less disturbing end. He lived well into old age fading very gradually until it became clear that the kindest thing for him was to help him on his way. Taking him to the vet for the very last time was almost unbearably sad but his death was calm and peaceful. He had enjoyed a good, long life and his departure was the best it could be. He had what I later learned could be described as "a good death".

A further experience of pet loss hit me many years later long after these childhood losses had become a distant memory and I was taken completely by surprise by the depth and force of my grief which matched anything I had experienced in the wake of my human losses.

There are many who play down pet loss because they don't understand it. It seems that there is a largely unspoken hierarchy of loss by which bereavements are ranked according to the level of grief they are likely to generate and the loss of an animal comes right at the very bottom of this hierarchy. But this did not match with what I was experiencing when we lost our beautiful cairn terrier, Bobby, and it created in me an anxiety that my feelings were somehow abnormal and so needed to be kept hidden.

I started searching the internet for information on pet bereavement. What I was really looking for was permission to feel what I was feeling without having to consider myself a freak and, fortunately for my sanity, I found it. It gradually became clear that there were many people who shared and understood my feelings completely.

Dog lovers have known for a very long time the strength of the bond that can form between dogs and humans and there is now scientific evidence which goes some way towards explaining this. Research has discovered that when dogs stare into human eyes, oxytocin is activated in both human and dog. Oxytocin is a hormone that plays a significant role in maternal bonding and trust.

This bonding is further cemented by the way our lives are interwoven with our dogs. Bobs was stitched into the very fabric of my existence almost without me realising it. It was just the way life was. He came into our home as a puppy when I had ceased formal work and he changed it gradually and subtly for ever. He was my constant companion. We got up together, went to bed together and took a long daily walk together. I was almost completely responsible for his survival and well being so it was up to me to keep him healthy and safe. No wonder that I should be so grief stricken when I lost him in traumatic circumstances. I began to realise that it would have been more abnormal not to be so devastated and so I write my experience in total honesty refusing to be silenced by people wishing to suggest that my grief was in excess of what I had lost, for they have no understanding at all of what it was exactly that I had lost. Bobby was way, way more to me than the reductive phrase "only a dog" might suggest. He was not just any old dog, easily replaceable. He was special, unique with his own individual character.

My partner, John, my brother, Dave and I were on holiday on the Llyn Peninsular in the village of Llanbedrog. Our cottage was lovely, close to the sea and the weather which had been wet, grey and miserable for some time had brightened into warmth and sunshine which was the forecast for the whole week. It seemed as though some benevolent force was looking after us making us feel blessed. Little did we know then what was in store for us.

Day three of our holiday dawned bright and sunny as predicted and we set off to explore Morfa Nefyn which turned out to be a dramatic and beautiful place. We strolled along the beach and then, leaving the crowds behind, struck out along the coast path dropping down into a secluded cove for lunch. We paused for some time drinking in the beauty and tranquillity of the place, oblivious to the fact that lurking beneath this beautiful surface was something malevolent that was to rip away our joy and smash it into a thousand pieces.

As we made our way back across the beach in the late afternoon, we saw a woman fall awkwardly on the rocks. She was clearly quite badly hurt and it alerted us to the potential danger of the place although we failed to see it as the omen it turned out to be.

Back at the cottage the first signs of our tragedy began to unfold as Bob refused his dinner. This was most unlike him. He was very food motivated and rarely missed an opportunity to indulge his appetite. It was usually only sickness that prevented him from eating and this turned out to be the case. He was terribly sick and taking him outside it became apparent that he also had severe diarrhoea. It was not the first time this had happened and so, although I felt sad for the poor little chap, I was not unduly concerned and I took him to bed at our usual time.

However, what was unusual was that he awoke us around 3.00 am in obvious discomfort and, despite walks outside and our full attention, he failed to settle.

My concern began to grow and around 4.00 am I convinced John to call an emergency vet. At home I would have known how to proceed but not so here. It seemed that the only advice we got was to stop Bob drinking in order to stop the vomit reflex and to take him into the vets the following morning if he was no better. I was surprised that it had not been suggested that he see a vet right away either by having them call or by taking him in but I assumed this was not an option here. I don't know why I made that assumption but it has haunted me ever since. Why did we not insist that he see someone there and then? Had we done that could anything have been done which would have ensured a more positive outcome? We will never know but the question fuels a sense of guilt in me which persists to this day.

The night seemed endless. Bob paced ceaselessly around the unfamiliar cottage and by the morning he seemed no better so off we went to the vets. We didn't have to wait long to be seen and the vet assured us that all Bob's vital signs were normal. Administering an anti sickness injection, she assured us that he would be feeling much better in a couple of hours so we returned to the cottage confident that Bob was on the way to recovery. And so it seemed.

We had put up a crate covered in blankets so that he had a safe and private place if he wanted it. He crawled in there and settled down quietly while I went for a shower to revive myself after the sleepless night, feeling hugely relieved that the anxiety of that night was over and normality had been restored.

We left Bob in his crate for quite some time. He had spent the previous day walking and had been up for most of the night so we knew he must be exhausted and needing to rest. I kept glancing at him and he looked peaceful and settled . I do not know how long it was before I bent down to give him a thorough check.

"Bob doesn't seem to be breathing," I said but even as I said the words I didn't believe them. John looked and claimed that he had seen movement but I remained unconvinced as I touched him and he remained motionless. I then uttered the words, "I think he's gone," but I wasn't really connecting with the reality of what I was saying and if I had been I would not have believed it to be true.

John then tried to rouse him but failing to do so he lifted him out of the crate and confirmed my very worst fears. "Yes, I think he has," he responded as he lay Bob's lifeless body back down.

For a moment time seemed to stand still as I stared in disbelief at Bob's immobile body desperately willing it to move, to show some sign of life, give out some sign of hope no matter how small but there was nothing. He just lay there where John had placed him - stone still.

As I reached out to touch him it felt as though his little body had already begun to stiffen suggesting that he had been dead for some time. My beautiful, little cairn terrier had been lying in his crate dead and I had been obliviously engaged in routine tasks feeling only a sense of relief that he was on the mend. The thought was unbearable and sent the vicious talons of grief ripping through me releasing an uncontrollable torrent of tears.

In that instant grief consumed me. Even now as I write, a part of me feels embarrassed at the strength of my feelings as if I should apologise for it but at that moment the feelings were just as powerful as those experienced in response to human loss. It felt as though everything had been snatched from me: present contentment and any chance of future happiness as well as any ability to think straight or act rationally and as the physical pain of it subsided I was left with a sense of complete and utter desolation. No description of grief ever comes close to the suffocating reality of it.

I have no idea how long these feelings lasted but I do know that very gradually practicalities began to assert themselves. I knew that things needed to be done but I was at a loss to know what those things were. I had never been in this situation before and we were far from home surrounded by the unfamiliar. It slowly dawned on me that our holiday needed to be brought to a premature end and somehow we needed to get Bob's small body back home with us, to lay him to rest where he belonged not here on the Llyn Peninsular which was feeling like a hostile place where malevolent spirits lurked behind rocks and in obscure corners just waiting to strike.

I called the vets to let them know that Bob had died within hours of their misdiagnosis. They offered to store his body overnight and I made a further call to make arrangements to take him the following day to a pet crematorium back home.

From that point on I seemed to be operating on auto-pilot, struggling to take in what had happened. How was it possible that our small dog could be perfectly healthy, full of energy and enjoying life one minute and hours later be dead? It was inconceivable and every fibre of my being was fighting against the unalterable reality of it while at the same time robotically working through the practicalities that were necessary to collect Bob's body and get us all back home.

I found it impossible to eat and sleeping seemed like little more than snatched moments but somehow I got through the night, finished packing up the car and left behind the cottage where our tragedy had concluded. Any pleasure there may have been there had long since evaporated for us and I was glad to turn the key and leave it behind as we drove to the vets to collect Bob's body.

As the receptionist approached she asked us to wait outside by a side door. It was perfectly understandable that they did not wish to carry the dead body of a dog that had been in their care through a waiting room of pet owners whose pets were still very much alive. However, I had less understanding of the fact that we were kept waiting for quite some time before anyone appeared.

The sense of desolation as we stood outside that vets waiting to receive the lifeless body of our beautiful cairn terrier is indescribable. Though the sun was shining, it failed to warm me and I might as well have been surrounded by a frozen wasteland.

The vet who had treated Bob did not appear with the receptionist, although I had seen that she was around, and he was finally handed to John who placed him in his basket on the special platform we had made for him in the car. We had decided and ensured that he was not to be transported like an ordinary piece of luggage. This was very precious cargo and was to be treated as such.

And so began the long journey home. The contrast between the outward journey and this return could not have been greater. Bob's agile little body which had travelled down on my knee was now beside me and forever stilled. My expectations of a relaxing and enjoyable holiday were atrophied completely. We were a very subdued little group and barely a word was spoken between us for the entire cheerless journey.

Arriving back in Derby, we dropped Dave off and then made our way to Memorial Wood, the pet crematorium at Hoton. There we were welcomed by Rowan who completely understood the trauma of our loss and treated us with great warmth and kindness. John carried Bob inside where his wrappings were undone; he was placed in his basket on a large table and he was treated with dignity and respect.

It had all happened so suddenly and unexpectedly that we did not feel able to go straight ahead with the cremation. We needed time to absorb the loss and to consider how best to give him the send off he deserved and which would satisfy us. So we left him at Memorial Wood while we returned home and planned our farewell. It was the last thing we would do for him and so it had to be right.

Two days later we said our last goodbyes and Bob's body was finally returned to us as a small bag of ashes.

The avalanche of my tears could not come close to expressing how unbearably sad it was that this should be the end of Bob's way too short life and we left Memorial Wood clutching all that remained of our beautiful cairn terrier's little body and having only really taken the first step in coming to terms with our loss.

The house is full of reminders of Bob: the chair he loved to sit in; the sofa he loved to snooze on; the window seat that served as his look-out post from where he might observe any approaching danger especially alert to the approach of cat or squirrel. If either of these appeared he would literally scream as if being severely tortured, a sound which conveyed the extent of his frustration at his inability to get at this potential prey.

Then there is his empty basket in the corner of the bedroom; his drawers of toys and uneaten food and his favourite spots in the garden where he used to hide or soak up the sun or go looking for frogs. I catch glimpses of him out of the corner of my eye and hear the whimper he used when he wanted to be let back into the house. I am momentarily convinced that it is really him only to realise seconds later that it is just a fleeting illusion, a shadow no easier to grasp than Bob himself. I experience the impulse to do things for him such as putting out his food, getting ready to walk him or going through his bedtime routines. For a split second Bob is alive as the impulse bypasses reality but, of course, it doesn't last.

I feel that I let Bob down. It was up to me to keep him safe and I had failed monumentally. I am haunted by guilt as I go over and over the events as they unfolded. Was there anything I could have done to save Bob? Could I have insisted that he see a vet at 4.00 am when we first contacted them?

Should I have stressed the seriousness of his condition more forcefully? Was I in fact aware of the seriousness at that time? Should I have insisted that blood tests were taken? Did I know at the time that blood tests were needed? Did I trust the vet too much? Did Bob ingest something poisonous on the beach that day? If so, should I have been aware and prevented him? Or was it a pre-existing condition that just happened to flare up when we were on holiday and so less equipped to cope with it? Could it then have been something like pancreatitis and if so was I to blame for giving him too many cheese and sausage treats? And on and on and on. These thoughts taunt my waking hours, going round and round and round unanswered in my mind.

Maybe guilt is an inevitable part of bereavement which has to have its time, however long that might be, creating its disturbance until its energy is finally spent and the questions, even unresolved, can be laid to rest. Then all that's left is the excruciating sadness of Bob's absence and the unalterable truth that I will never again see Bob, never again stroke his beautiful, little body or chase him round the garden with his favourite blue bone. Nor will I ever again witness him presenting that same blue bone to welcome any visitors which was his long established routine. Wherever I look, there's a space where Bob once was and should still be.

I still need to exercise and stay active and at first I trace the steps that I used to walk with Bobs. Although it's profoundly sad, there is some comfort in it. I see the familiar dog walkers who all seem to understand the trauma of losing Bob the way I have. I do, however, feel a little lost without him and find myself quickening my pace in order to catch up with cute looking dogs especially if they look anything like a cairn, as if I can somehow get back something of my Bob which, of course, I can't. It feels as though there's something slightly mad in this behaviour as if I am in the grip of something stronger than me and over which I have no control.

Gradually the new normal begins to assert itself. I get up alone and get on with the day. There is no Bob to feed and no Bob to walk. John and I go to places we would not have gone to if Bob had still been with us but he slips into our conversations and we discover that in a sense we take him with us and that, while over time we may mention him less, he will always be with us. He was and will remain an important part of our lives.

Bob taught me many things; the possible joy in every moment and the satisfaction to be found in small things. And perhaps the most precious thing he taught me was that I was capable of loving a little cairn terrier unconditionally and able to put his needs above my own. I am only sorry that I was unable to nurture him through a much longer life. He was only seven and a half when he died; way, way too young.

Pet bereavement has much in common with human bereavement it seems. However, in contrast, the standard response to the loss of a dog is to ask whether you're going to have another one. Some believe it helps to ease the grief but I'm not sure about this for me. Part of me feels it would be a betrayal of Bob to have another dog too soon but maybe in time it will feel right. If we should have another, it will be down to the fact that our experience with Bob was so very positive and so a fitting legacy. We will have to see.

Terror on the Streets

Survivors aren't always the strongest; sometimes they're
the smartest but more often simply the luckiest.
Carrie Ryan: "The Dark and Hollow Places"

It was 1974. I was eighteen years old and I had just left home for the very first time to become a student.

My parents kept quite strict tabs on me while I was growing up always demanding to know where I was going, who I was going with and what time I would be back and there was always, always a curfew which I failed to meet at my peril.

So leaving home for me was exciting, it was liberating, it was FREEDOM! But it was also slightly scary and one night in November was way more frightening than that. It was nothing short of terrifying and I can taste the fear of it still.

My heart starts to quicken at the thought of it as I am transported back to that November evening which began pretty much like every other evening since leaving home with plans to meet up with friends in town in one of the student pubs. My priority at that time was to socialise and generally enjoy life without a curfew. It had little to do with studying or self improvement.

Time was getting on. If I didn't get a move on my friends might move on without me and so, pulling on my boots and grabbing my shawl (it was the 70s remember) I made for the door of the student quarters. It was then that I heard the first whispers of "bombs", "explosions", "injuries" and "deaths". It all sounded rather dramatic and unlikely so at first I thought nothing of it but as I made my way down the stairs I became aware of unusual crowds of students moving in my direction. They seemed to be fleeing from something rather than heading for anywhere special. Their movements seemed edgy and their talk breathless and unnaturally fast.

Something was definitely amiss and as I stepped outside I heard the urgent wail of a siren closely followed by another and another until the night was split with a wailing cacophony proclaiming disaster on a very large scale. Whatever had happened must be pretty serious I thought. Perhaps there was something real about the talk of "bombs", "explosions" and "injuries" that I had heard earlier. Would it be foolish to persevere with my plans and head into the confusion of siren noise and flashing lights? I felt the beginning of a slow panic starting in my chest and playing out in my head with a chaos of barely formed questions. What should I do? Where should I go?

Those immediate decisions were made for me as a uniformed police officer appeared saying, "The town centre is closed. Turn back. Stay calm. There is no need to panic". I admired his steady composure but did not in the least believe him. Who ever heard of a town centre being closed? All of my senses were telling me that there was every need to panic so I turned and stumbled back up the stairs heading for some kind of safety from whatever dark menace was loose on those streets.

Safely back in the shared kitchen area, students were gathering in various states of disarray many breathless and desperate to recount what they had witnessed. Outside the sirens continued to wail, the lights to flash and the injured to arrive back some limping, some in bandages and some clearly very disturbed.

In those fractured moments it was difficult to work out exactly what was happening. Information was gathered in fragments as people rattled out what they had seen. Anxiety fed off itself and tensions increased, discharged in volleys of unfocused monologues. Chaos! There was chaos – inside and out!

It very gradually became possible to grasp what was happening. Unlikely though it seemed, bombs were exploding across Birmingham city centre. They really were. Several had gone off shattering everything and everyone in close proximity. People had died, no-one knew how many, many were injured, no-one knew how many and no-one knew where the next explosion might be.

It occurred to me that I should probably call my parents who had no idea where I was, who I was with and when I would be home. I was on the loose in Birmingham with no curfew and I should perhaps at least let them know that I was unharmed. But I wasn't alone in thinking that way and the queues for the phones (no mobiles then) were impossibly long, snaking round corridors and way out of sight. The call would have to wait until tomorrow.

It was a very long night and people did not begin to disperse until the early hours. As I returned to the solitude of my room I pondered the events of the evening; dramatic, extreme, devastating. I found it hard to make sense of what I had witnessed. Over time it was revealed that the bombs were planted by the IRA; twenty one people lost their lives and many, many more were injured. I struggled to make a connection between the innocent victims of those bombs and events in Northern Ireland, anything that might provide some kind of justification for the acts of carnage but I could find nothing.

The repercussions of that terrible night have reverberated down the years. A chain of events was set in motion to which as yet, almost forty five years later, there has been no resolution.

That night I learnt that death can suddenly explode from the shadows in a shock of violence and chaos claiming its victims in apparently random fashion and having lasting and terrible consequences for everyone in its orbit.

Initiation

To live in hearts we leave/ Is not to die.
Thomas Campbell: "Hallowed Ground"

It was some years after this that I was finally initiated into the adult world of funerals. The funeral was that of my young cousin so a particularly tragic occasion but I don't think I would have attended if my father had not been unable to go. I think my parents still saw it as the prerogative of the older generation, that they should be the family representatives until they were no longer able to be.

Well, on this occasion my Dad was unwell and so it fell to me to accompany my Mum. This cousin had been fairly distant in adult life but, nevertheless, I found the occasion enormously affecting not least in seeing the grief etched into the faces of my Uncle Jack and Aunt Margaret and which seemed to stoop their bodies as if they carried a physical weight.

It felt as though death was getting ever closer and one Saturday afternoon in February 1994 the very thing I had been unable to imagine as a child became reality.

Do Not Go Gentle Into That Good Night

Mostly it is loss which teaches us about
the worth of things.
Arthur Shopenhauer

As I recall it was a sunny day but windy. Dad was in the final throes of terminal cancer which had gradually sucked the life from his body. He had only been diagnosed three months previously so it seemed a fairly swift deterioration. I vividly remember the day he went to collect the results of his bronchoscopy. He insisted that he wanted to go alone and so the rest of the family were left to their silent prayers, or whatever method they chose, to get them through the excruciating business of waiting. I tried distraction but it didn't seem to work for me. I was at work teaching English Literature to teenage boys but the uncertainty of Dad's diagnosis buzzed around in my brain all day. When Mum phoned in the evening the worst possible diagnosis was confirmed. Dad had terminal cancer. There was nothing that could be done. At first I heard it only in my ears and only gradually did its full significance permeate throughout the rest of my body finally taking up residence deep, deep inside like a canker at my very core.

When I actually spoke to Dad himself he sought to make light of it. He pointed out that we are all terminal which, of course, we are but since we all so often tend to live as if we are not, there is something profoundly different about being given it as a medical prognosis.

In our society death is rarely spoken of: the subject borders on the taboo and this fact was painfully evident in our family as we all strived to come to terms with Dad's diagnosis. I think perhaps we were in denial and so chose to maintain silence on the subject and carry on with life as if nothing had changed. For all our efforts to cling to normality, however, the fact of Dad's impending death was always on the fringes of my consciousness and occasionally received acknowledgement in an indirect sort of way.

It was his habit to clean my car whenever I visited . We are not a very demonstrative family and this was his way of demonstrating his continuing care and concern for me. So on one of my visits Dad, although visibly fragile, picked up his sponge and went out to clean my car. He carelessly dripped dirty water down the front of his outdoor jacket and started to berate himself for this. Meanwhile Mum had appeared at the door and immediately said, "It doesn't matter. We need to get you a new jacket anyway."

Dad raised an eyebrow and gave a wry smile that spoke volumes. Mum's comment suggested an ongoing life that needed a decent outdoor jacket. Dad's reaction registered a question whether this was, in fact, the case.

How long exactly was Mum expecting him to live? How long could he expect to live? Would it be long enough to justify the cost of a brand new jacket? Was Mum completely unaware of these questions or was she skating around them for Dad's benefit or for her own? Questions, questions all unspoken.

On another occasion the family was gathered around the television watching a crime drama. One of the crooks snarled at another who had double crossed him, the worst fate he could think of which was, "I hope you die of cancer!"

The shock in the room was palpable but no-one spoke. The curse had writ large the severity of the sentence that Dad was suffering and I felt our silence left him out there somewhere on his own. We were unable to find the words to accompany him.

I remember arriving one day with a plant pot full of early daffodils to brighten Dad's sick room: beautiful, yellow trumpets heralding the imminent arrival of Spring. Spring, the season of new life. I wanted to cheer Dad up but on reflection I think I was probably in denial about the reality of his situation. And anyway, I would have had no idea what to do to help my much loved Dad as he lay dying.

Scenes such as this came back to haunt me once he had died. My sense of guilt was visceral as I realised that while he was surrounded by his family, he was in many ways very alone with his suffering. But this is jumping ahead.

Death is the one thing in life that is guaranteed and yet we receive no guidance in how to face it so when I received a phone call from Mum, just a few months after Dad's terminal diagnosis, to say that we were about to lose him and I should make my way to Derby, the call came as a total shock. I replaced the receiver and sat in a strange silence while I tried to digest the information and organise my scrambled thoughts to work out the practicalities of packing. What would I need for this event? I had no idea. In fact I found it impossible to think beyond the long journey ahead and arriving at my parents' front door. What would be the other side of that door? I wondered.

So it was that in a state of complete disorganisation, I got behind the wheel of my Vauxhall Corsa and set off for my destination. Fragmented and disturbing thoughts rushed through my mind. What if I didn't make it? What if he died before I got there? What if I never saw my Dad alive again? These thoughts fuelled my instinct to press hard down on the accelerator and go just as fast as I possibly could but a voice that seemed almost not my own calmed this instinct.

The journey seemed interminable and it was a massive relief to arrive at that front door. And beyond it was my Mum and a strange kind of routine with my Dad on his deathbed at its centre. Bedding was changed at regular intervals; food offered and refused; liquid taken in the most painful of sips and lips kept moist with cotton wool sticks. Toilet trips were major expeditions in which the two of us would shoulder the weight of Dad's helpless body across the landing to the bathroom, a slow and exhausting trip where followed the awkward and humiliating business of emptying bladder and bowels. As the days passed even this became impossible and these needs too had to be catered for in bed: images which over the years I have sought with some success to bury.

Visits from District Nurses and other health professionals broke up the days and reassured us that we were coping okay. On his last visit the Doctor's words, "There's nothing more I can do," crashed down on me like stones and lodged in my stomach where they seemed to take up residence. The words were so final and unequivocal. Nothing could have signalled the end with greater clarity.

During these days my brother Dave at first coped by clinging desperately to his own routine. He continued doggedly to go to work and to return at his usual times. He still lived with our parents so in some ways his normality was less disrupted than mine. However, it meant that so far he had been far more involved than me and had witnessed Dad's decline close up. He had felt the weight of Dad's diseased body as he had had to carry him up the stairs in a poignant enactment of role reversal. "The child is father of the man".

But now Mum and I were providing round the clock care and were becoming exhausted by it when there was an unexpected ring on the doorbell. There on the step stood my eldest brother, Steve, and his partner, Maureen. Steve was a frequently absent family member. Often we would hear nothing of him for weeks and months on end and at one point the silence had stretched across years until I had actually set off to physically track him down. I've never really known what those absences were about. But that is his story to tell not mine.

Steve's initial greeting was full of life and bluster. He was confident that Dad would pull through simply because Dad was Dad and he always did. He was a fighter who we had never seen beaten by anything. He had made it through a world war as one of the youngest sergeants in the airforce serving in Burma among other places and witnessing untold atrocities. He had learnt to "put on a brave face in front of the troops" at an early age and that was how we were used to seeing him.

However, I must have had the reality of the present situation stamped across my features because the heartiness of Steve's greeting instantly evaporated and the colour bleached from his face. "How's things?" he said as he struggled to grasp the new reality. It wasn't a question that he really wanted answering: it was put to bridge the enormous gap that had opened up between the reality he had anticipated and the brutality of the one he now faced. But before he had really had time to digest it, he swung into a whirlwind of activity seeing what needed to be done and doing it.

First on the list was a meal for us all. While we had been attending to Dad's needs we had been carelessly neglecting our own so we were massively grateful as all five of us sat down at the table to eat: subdued but together, united in our focus. And then a make-shift rota was established in which we all played our part in looking after Dad. Steve and Maureen were on the night watch and crawled exhausted into beds the rest of us vacated to take up the day shifts.

During those last few days my world shrunk almost to the four walls of my parents' house, my childhood home where Dad's every need was being immediately met. Sometimes this meant venturing beyond those walls. Every such trip had a strange dreamlike quality. People appeared as distant figures in a completely different dimension. I felt as though I was moving through an underwater world in which it was impossible to reach out and grasp anything. It was incomprehensible how life seemed to be continuing as normal with people going about their business oblivious to the fact that a seismic shift was occurring in my life.

Inside the house we struggled to keep the wheels of ordinary existence turning: washing, cooking, eating and so on while ministering to the needs of my dad: needs vastly different to ours which now included the monitoring of a syringe drive automatically administering morphine and gradually taking him further and further from us to a world of drug psychosis and distorted reality.

Occasionally our worlds would collide with varying effects sometimes comic, sometimes poignant, sometimes both. At one point he suddenly pointed to something we were unable to see on the bed covers declaring it to be "three blind mice" dancing before him. Another time he must have sensed that he was nearing the end and called out for help. I rushed to his side anxious to supply whatever it was that might be needed but when I asked what that might be he said that it was, "Nothing physical". He was already beyond my help.

On another occasion all the family were working together under Dave's careful supervision to transfer Dad to a more comfortable mattress. It was a tricky manoeuvre and he awoke in the middle of it. His surprise amused us and we all laughed in unison. His response was to say, "I'll tell you lot something, this isn't bloody funny". These turned out to be his last words and he was right; it wasn't in the least bit "bloody funny".

At this point, his world and mine were vast distances apart. He was on his way to a place where the physical as we know it no longer existed, where he could leave behind his broken body and unlock life's mystery while I had not even started to prepare for living with his absence, living with the space where once he had sat, had laughed, had sung, had loved.

I had not started to come to terms with the truth that a man so strong, so capable, so totally dependable could be so physically reduced. As a small child I adored my Dad. He really was my hero; strong, capable and utterly dependable. He would lift me up and swing me round with ease and he would walk me along with my bare feet on top of his in order to protect me from the cold of lino floors.

At this time I was frightened to go upstairs at night because the lights in the hallway cast the shadow of what looked to me like a witch's hat. How could this not be frightening? Dad would patiently stand at the foot of the stairs shouting up reassuringly until I had completed the expedition and returned downstairs to safety. How brave was my Dad? He wasn't even frightened of witches and their malevolent spells.

On seaside family holidays he was always there supervising the building of sand castles with their intricate waterways and paper flags and braving the cold waters of the North Sea making sure that we all stayed safe and did not get swept away by the sea's uncaring currents.

It was Dad who took control of things the day I felt myself hurtling uncontrollably into the jaws of my own death.

My brothers and I had been playing outside and Mum had called us in for lunch. Steve had issued a challenge declaring that the last one to touch Mum was a fool and we both set off at full speed anxious not to be the loser and the fool.

We reached the french window leading into the dining room at the same time trying to shove each other to one side in our attempts to be the victor. But suddenly it all went horribly wrong as there was the awful sound of smashing glass and I realised that I had put my arm through one of the small window panes shattering glass all over the place. I was stunned and anxious as I waited for the inevitable reprimand and punishment. But that wasn't what happened.

Mum came rushing in from the kitchen demanding to know what was going on . I started to stammer out an explanation and an apology which was immediately interrupted by a totally unexpected scream from Mum followed closely by her question, "What on earth have you done to your arm?"

It was at this point that I realised that I had ripped my flesh on the lethal shards of glass and blood seemed to be everywhere; my blood. I was petrified, convinced that the only possible outcome of this event was death; my death. Surely it was not possible to lose so much blood and still be able to stand upright and function as a human being – no certainly this must be the end for me.

I remember screaming literally for my life unable to stop, my cries filling the house and the surrounding neighbourhood striking a note of pure dread, I later learnt, into all who heard me. A clean pillowcase was put over my arm both to protect my wound and to limit the spread of blood but it also served to emphasise the seriousness of the situation as its clean whiteness gradually turned blood red. I was plied with hot, very sweet tea but remained inconsolable.

It was at this point that Dad took control. His voice stayed calm and measured as he called for a taxi to take us to the hospital. Five minutes later when the taxi had not arrived, I heard him repeat the call explaining that the situation was an emergency and that we needed the taxi urgently.

Hearing the word "emergency" from my Dad's lips filled me with renewed panic. If calm, unflappable Dad saw the situation as an emergency then things must be desperate indeed. Fortunately within minutes the car arrived and we were on our way. Throughout the journey Dad appeared calm and reassuring and he delivered me safely to the hospital operating theatre where I was put back together with twenty stitches and plenty of TLC from the hospital staff.

I don't think we ever knew who was the last to touch Mum but I certainly felt it was me who was the fool. It felt as though I had been snatched from the jaws of imminent death and Dad had been a key player in the rescue.

All these things made it not surprising that when ever he went overseas, which he was forced to do from time to time, I missed him terribly and cried over the absence of "my wonderful daddy". All these things were so at odds with Dad's present reduced state.

The actual moment of Dad's passing remains frozen in time. Mum had gone to lie down, exhausted with the weight of all she had been carrying for weeks. Steve was in the garden digging furiously, no longer able to face the reality of approaching death, digging as if solace were to be unearthed in the soil somewhere. Maureen was busy with domestic concerns; cleaning, cooking and generally keeping things going. I lay on the floor at the foot of Dad's bed aching for sleep but reluctant to leave him. Dave alone was by his bedside keeping watch and he alone witnessed the moment balanced between life and death, the ceasing of breath, the total stillness. I heard him say, "I think he's gone" and I rose from the floor to confirm the truth of this.

He had certainly gone, in that he had stopped breathing but I felt strongly that some part of him was still around. I cannot give a rational explanation of that feeling but nevertheless I think that was why I rushed to waken mum so that she could be with him before he fully disappeared and, for the same reason, Steve was called to lay down his spade.

Maybe it would have been comforting to have some ready made rituals to navigate me across the chasm that had opened up before me. Victorians, for example, would stop the clocks, draw the curtains and cover the mirrors. I could well understand the urge to stop the clocks for time did indeed seem to stop for a while as each one of us retreated into our own private leave taking. I felt the rise and fall of my own breath through which came crashing a sudden and all consuming experience of desolation – an emptiness so complete that it quickly gave way to panic and an overwhelming ache to just have my Dad back. This was the inconceivable abandonment envisaged in childhood.

But it wasn't to last as the moment was interrupted by the unexpected arrival of my Aunt Margaret, Dad's sister, who had been a regular visitor throughout Dad's illness and whose response to what she found was to smother emotion and leap to take control of the practicalities. The silence was replaced with the clatter of activity as undertakers were called; the deathbed stripped; sheets washed and the various paraphernalia of Dad's illness dismantled. Finally Dad left home in a stark black body bag.

The next day the District Nurses arrived to take away the unused medical supplies. It felt as though all the signs of Dad's existence were being stripped away just as if he had never been and my experience of this was visceral. I heard the keening sound of a wounded animal and was shocked to realise the noise was emanating from deep within me. The icy fingers of disapproval from the rest of the family reached out and silenced my grief. In my family emotion is closely policed, caged out of harm's way.

But everything that was happening felt strangely unconnected to what was happening in me almost as if it were taking place in some other dimension.

This feeling of dislocation was magnified when a couple of days later I found myself with Mum and Dave at the Funeral Directors leafing through glossy catalogue pages to select a coffin from the myriad ones available. The choice was overwhelming. There was a coffin to suit every possible taste and wallet. Death it seems has been well and truly commercialised. Was this what had replaced the rituals of bygone days? As if death can somehow be branded and packaged and comfort found in the patient explanation of the pros and cons of the various coffins on offer.

This collision of vastly different perspectives struck us all at the same moment as bizarre and our spontaneous collective response was to laugh uncontrollably for what seemed to be a very long time. It released some tension but it did nothing to help me absorb the reality of Dad's passing and I was left with the inexplicable feeling that I would somehow see my Dad again. So it was that some days later, against all the advice, I made my way to the chapel of rest and there I saw that he had really gone, in a way that he had not when he first passed away.

He lay in his coffin silent and so so still, not a breath, not a flicker. I reached out to touch his cold unyielding flesh, shocked at the marble deadness of it. And there were his hands: hands that had spent a lifetime in busyness - making and fixing broken things; digging, planting and cutting back; now so still – forever still.

Random images of those hands in action flashed through my mind: mending lawn mowers and washing machines; making fireplaces, bookshelves and tables as well as a model farm and a fort as Christmas gifts for my brothers. I remembered him once unravelling for me the twisted links of a very intricate chain. His eyesight was fading and so he devised a Heath Robinson contraption to hold a magnifying glass which allowed him to properly see and then release the knots. He wasn't going to be beaten by fading eyesight. He was always resourceful and in short what people described as "good with his hands".

But now I saw that a white handkerchief had been placed in his hands – a flag of surrender? The final defeat? Whoever placed it there could not have known what they did.

I had been advised not to make this visit but I was glad that I did. I had been nursing a secret and unsettling feeling that somehow I would see my Dad again but the visit made clear that he had gone: unequivocally departed in a way that I felt he had not when he took his final breath.

The next big event was the funeral and oddly clothes seemed to acquire a new significance. Dad was not a materialistic man. He was not overly impressed by external appearances. In fact I recall an occasion when Mum had gone away for a few days and Dad decided to decorate the living room as a surprise for her. He was painting the ceiling in the centre of which was a smashed light fitting. I pointed out that he should really replace this and he agreed. But then his painting arm dropped to his side and with a deep sigh he proclaimed, "But what have you got when you've done it? Just another bloody lampshade". I could sort of see his point.

Not materialistic then but he did believe in looking smart. I think this came from his days in the RAF as did his insistence on highly polished shoes, not only for himself but for all of us. Every school night Dad would instruct us to get our shoes which he would then vigorously polish until you could, "See your face in 'em". So it was that we all felt a very strong desire to look smart at Dad's funeral. This was probably the reason that Mum had been so anxious to have a new coat.

She had been fretting that she didn't have a decent coat to wear to the funeral and so it was that a few days after Dad's death the two of us made our way into Derby town centre to look for a new one. A strange thing happened as we got into the car. When I switched on the ignition the needles on all the gauges seemed to be engaged in some kind of bizarre and random dance, bobbing around furiously in all directions. This must have lasted for a couple of minutes before they settled back into normality.

I have no idea what caused this phenomenon but remain convinced that it was in some way connected to my Dad's passing. Was he with us in some form and this his way of communicating that? Perhaps. I'm certainly not ruling it out.

Normality restored, it was off to find Mum's coat. For Dad's funeral only the best would do and on this occasion the best was Brindleys, a department store that had been in the same family for years, noted for quality and exclusivity, as exclusive as Mum was ever going to be able to afford anyway.

I had to admire this little woman having lost a partner of well over forty years, struggling with grief but striding purposefully into Brindleys in order to do Dad proud on his last big day. The coat was chosen, shortened and collected later that week.

I meanwhile decided that I needed to do a two hundred mile round trip home to collect my clothes for Dad's farewell. It turned out to be a more eventful journey than I would have wished. Accompanied by a close friend I set off and all was going well until the road began to feel unusually bumpy and the car was refusing to respond to the dipping of the accelerator. As these conditions persisted, I decided to pull over onto the hard shoulder to investigate. Having slowed to a halt we got out of the car to investigate and it didn't take long to realise that one of the back tyres was completely shredded. The policeman who came to our rescue gave voice to the very real danger we had been in, pointing out just how lucky we were to be in one piece. Wheel changed we continued on our way with no further mishaps and the mission was completed successfully.

Maybe a guardian spirit had looked down on us that day and decided that the family had as much grief as it could manage for now and so had wrapped us in its embrace in order to forestall any further tragedy; a random act of charity in an otherwise indifferent universe.

We still needed to decide what Dad should wear. He was, after all, the star of the show. Steve suggested a sports jacket and trousers, his normal informal but smart attire. Should one be smart but informal to depart this life? Mum didn't think so and I was in agreement with her. She thought the idea macabre. Dad had crossed the borderline to a place where clothes were no longer relevant. It was pointless for us to try to hold onto him by clothing him in our limited under-standing of how things are. As Hamlet says, "There's more things in heaven and earth, Horatio than are dreamt of in our philosophy". And so it was that a plain white funeral shroud was chosen for Dad's final departure.

I did hear of a young woman who was buried in her wedding dress. It put me in mind of Miss Haversham and I wondered why that choice had been made. Was it an attempt to preserve for ever, as if in aspic, what was understood to be the happiest day of her life – an eternal wedding?

Dad's funeral was on the 14th February, Valentine's Day. My Mum was bidding farewell to the man who for so many years had been her Valentine. It was many years later, after the death of my Mum that I discovered the evidence of this. Sorting through the contents of her dressing table, nestled at the very back of a drawer, I discovered a pile of handwritten letters held together with a pink ribbon.

These were private letters, intimate and precious written by my Dad to my Mum long before I was born. They had been secretly treasured through the ups and downs of their long years of marriage and really were no business of mine. My curiosity, however, was too strong to be silenced and so I unloosened the ribbon to set free the secrets it had for years kept safe.

The writing was unbearably tender and heartfelt. Here was my Dad as I had never known him; romantic and in love. I felt like an intruder trespassing in forbidden territory. These letters now are tied together once more and at the back of a different drawer. What will become of them when I am gone? Who will treasure them? Who will care?

That February Day in 1994 my Mum was saying goodbye to the writer of those letters while I was saying goodbye to my Dad: my Dad who had quite simply throughout my entire life always been there. So many memories of him played across my mind.

When I was about ten years old I was promised a piano and so it was that Dad and I made our way to view one that we had seen advertised in the local paper. It was a snowy day and we walked in the bitter cold across fields that are no longer there to a house in Spondon. As we were led inside, I was hoping against hope that the piano would meet with Dad's approval and, when we walked into the lounge and saw it, I could barely contain my excitement.

Dad had his own inimitable way of playing the instrument which he described as "knocking out a tune". Knocking was a particularly apt description as he would make octaves picking out the tune with his right hand and keeping a thumping bass rhythm with his left in which the actual notes were almost irrelevant. So on this day he sat down to give the instrument a test run. It seemed to pass muster. The deal was concluded and I was beyond excited as we set off on the long walk back home.

I had wanted a piano for so long that it seemed almost magical that I had finally got one, made even more so when Dad told me that the lounge we had been in was oddly familiar. He felt that he had been in it before and it had gradually dawned on him that it had been in a dream. The room had appeared to him exactly as it was except instead of an upright piano there was a full orchestra complete with grand piano. Dreams have no regard for scale.

He was overwhelmingly a man of logic, a trained engineer. "We're all carburettors and swearwords," he sometimes joked. He had no time for "fancy thinking", by which he meant anything that did not have a scientific explanation so the revelation of this dream was rather startling.

More prosaically was the fact that he taught me to read and write. One day he placed a newspaper in front of me and asked me what the headline said. I didn't have a clue. Up until this point I had managed to fool my parents with various tricks into believing that I could read and write but my cover was blown and it was deemed to be a serious matter. "Mona, our Gillian can't read," Dad shouted to Mum in the kitchen. "Nonsense, she's a lovely little reader," Mum shouted back but Dad knew better and it was a situation that he was determined to rectify.

I put my lack of progress in this area down to my teacher, Mrs Atwell. I will never forget Mrs Atwell. She squats toad-like in my memory. I can still hear her rasping voice and feel the inward shrink of humiliation she loved to inflict. I was frightened of her and I was right to be. She was queen of the classroom which she ruled with an iron rod. There were the clever ones, her favourites, who could do no wrong and then there were we lesser beings, her loathed ones who could do no right and I became too fearful to even try. Much safer to copy the work of those who knew how than to flounder and struggle alone.

But she always knew did Mrs Atwell and my misguided initiative was severely punished. In memory it feels like I spent hours standing in disgrace by Mrs Atwell's desk consumed by the crawling heat of shame; mute. And what did it teach me? Fear and the ingenuity not to get caught, to strive for invisibility.

Had it been left to Mrs Atwell, I doubt whether I would ever have learnt to read and write. Thankfully it was not. And so began Dad's private lessons. He set up a make shift classroom with a small desk and blackboard and he systematically lead me through the twenty six letters of the alphabet. His teaching methods were old fashioned and somewhat pedestrian but over time they worked.

When he asked me a question I was unable to answer, one of my brothers would whisper it through and then with a stern word from Dad they would be immediately dismissed from the room for the duration of my lesson. Gradually I began to appreciate the magical transformation that occurs when letters are joined together. It was then that my love of books and reading was born and it has stayed with me ever since. Without Dad's patience and perseverance I may never have discovered that pleasure.

Then there was the family day out to London. The itinerary was meticulously planned in advance and on the day executed with military precision. It remains in my memory a kaleidoscope of impressions: Houses of Parliament, Big Ben, London Bridge, Tower Bridge, Crown Jewels, St Paul's, Westminster Abbey and more. By the time we boarded the train home, we had seen as much of London as was comfortably possible in one day.

Things, however, were not always quite so harmonious. We were not The Waltons and certainly had our fair share of conflict. Teenagers often need something to rebel against, I think, and for me Dad was a prime target. Retrospectively I think it was probably because I sensed he was sufficiently robust to withstand it and so during my teenage years we were often at war. To me then he represented authority and the social order. It was the 1970 s and it seemed that the entire younger generation was in pitched battle with the establishment. My naïve political ideology fuelled much of my protest and complaint but there were also the shackles of parental restraint which I experienced as unfairly restrictive and which I constantly challenged.

Memories, memories, so many memories: an avalanche threatening to crush the breath out of me and render me incapable of living through the day ahead.

How can one day do justice to all that makes up the life of a man? How can one short service be enough to wrap up a life and send the body, all that's left, on its way: a thirty minute allotted slot at the crematorium – in at the front door and out at the back, careful to be well out of sight before the arrival of the next body. The conveyor belt of death which we can be sure is never going to stop.

That February day was bitterly cold, grey and damp with persistent drizzle, external conditions reflecting my inner world. The morning was spent in domestic preparations for the funeral tea. Sandwiches were made and trifles. Home made cakes were spread out on a pure white table cloth with tea cups, plates and cutlery. The yardstick against which everything was measured was whether or not it would meet with Dad's approval while in reality he was the one person we could guarantee would not be there. Everyone pitched in with the preparations. It gave us something to do and took our attention away from the big black hole where Dad once was.

Domestic preparations completed, we donned our smart clothes. I completed my outfit with a string of opals which my Aunt Margaret had given me a few days after Dad's death informing me that they had been bought by my Dad in India for his mother many years ago. As I fastened the opals around my neck I had a strong sense of my Dad as someone's son just as

I was his daughter – life's recurring cycles. The finality embodied in the day somehow brought things into sharper focus, presenting a heightened awareness and reality.

The day was moving on and so it was that at one o'clock I looked out of my bedroom window to see the hearse arrive. "Dad's here," I shouted and the thought speared through me that Dad had arrived to the home he loved and was about to leave for the very last time. That moment of total recognition remains frozen in my consciousness. For a while all activity seemed suspended and then external reality reasserted itself as we all made our way to the waiting car.

We set off at walking pace, lead by the undertaker on foot wearing top hat and tails and carrying a silver topped cane. I thought this all seemed rather Dickensian and have since discovered that the custom does indeed have its roots in times before motor cars when coffins were transported by horse power. We, however, were automated and soon picked up pace.

I don't remember much about the actual funeral service but I do remember singing the one hymn we had chosen with all my available breath as if Dad's soul could take flight on the wings of my song.

I also remember Dad's coffin resting in front of us on a platform surrounded by open curtains which, at the end of the service, appeared to close themselves in a macabre kind of magic trick. In a traditional magic trick the curtains reopen to reveal some kind of miraculous transformation which was not going to happen here. The curtains shut us off from the final reality of death and we were lead outside.

At this point I was transported to Pashupatinath, a place I had visited some years earlier when travelling in Nepal. It is one of the most sacred Hindu temples in Nepal and lies on the banks of the Bagmati River on the outskirts of Kathmandu. They do death very differently there. People go there specifically to die and friends and relatives actively participate in all end of life care including the final disposal of the body. Complex rituals support the proceedings as the body is laid on a platform (ghat) especially constructed for a funeral pyre. I witnessed a family carrying their deceased, shrouded in a white sheet, towards a funeral pyre. The corpse was laid by the pyre and the sheet removed to reveal death in all its stark reality.

For me the sight was shocking but also strangely alluring. At that time I had not become intimate with death . I had only been acquainted at a distance and this corpse was up real close. I was entranced by its quiet nobility and its mystery.

I witnessed family members placing the deceased on the pyre and then a single member, most probably the oldest son, circled the body with a flaming torch which he then pushed into the mouth of the corpse in order to ignite it. And so the mourners directly witness the transformation from flesh to ashes.

Slightly downstream women do their washing and children laugh and play in the water. Life and death run side by side. This seems to be an honest acknow-ledgement of the relationship between them which in the west we strive to deny or avoid. It does seem to be true that, while death is the guaranteed destination for us all,we live for the most part as if we are immortal and as if we refuse to fully witness it, then we can proceed as if it does not exist.

At the time the scene triggered in me a depth of response I could not name; a sense of the connection of things, a continuity and a sense of something beyond physical reality, something which we might call the divine. It also evoked in me a profound admiration for a culture that could meet the reality of death head on in this way.

I have heard of the Muslim practice of a daughter washing the corpse of her mother and a son washing the corpse of his father in preparation for what comes next ; another ritual that involves direct interaction with the reality of death.

These practices appear to embody an ancient wisdom lost in the west where mourners are kept at a safe distance from death's reality. Death is boxed up and sanitised and we are left to make sense of it as best we can.

That morning back in England after the disappearance of the coffin, we were led back into the damp, grey outside world. The north wind knifed us through to our very bones and the bleak, desolate landscape served as a perfect reflection of how I was feeling. We stood around awkwardly making small talk with people some of whom we barely recognised. An old neighbour from some years previously stays in my mind possibly because she repeated the same performance on the occasion of my Mum's death. She talked and talked and talked to a point when I thought she would never stop and her talk was of all her family members, how well they were all doing, outlining in minute detail all their individual achievements on and on and on. And not once did she mention my Dad or make reference to how I might be feeling. We had just cremated my Dad. Was it really the right time to update me on the exploits of all her oh so healthy and successful family members? I think probably not.

Why is it that we are so inept around death and the bereaved? Society does not seem to acknowledge the enormity of it both for the deceased and those left behind. We're expected to be back at work within the week, "stiff upper lip," and all that.

So it is that the demands of every day life reassert themselves remarkably quickly. I remember my first day back at work. I was a teacher and we had just had half term. I was greeted in the car park by one of my colleagues who asked if I'd had a good holiday.

"Not really," I replied slightly taken aback by the question.

"Why's that?" he persisted.

"Well my Dad died," I said.

"Oh I know that but I mean apart from that," he blundered.

Totally shocked I searched for an appropriate response but failed to find one.

"There wasn't really any 'apart from that'," I whispered to his receding back as he ploughed ahead to his classroom.

So there I was straight back into the thick of things and digesting my loss was relegated to the pockets of time snatched between teaching, marking, lesson planning, reports, parents' evenings and the habitual routines of keeping body and soul functioning. It was often in the shadow of night that my grief emerged cloaked in dreams and nightmares. My Dad would appear but always just out of reach: swept away on an inexplicable tide or swallowed by the blackness of an impenetrable tunnel. In one dream I had the unsettling feeling that he was still alive and I was tortured with the problem of explaining this to people who had attended his funeral. Another night saw the circling of a flock of menacing, huge, black birds which I was desperately and unsuccessfully struggling to disperse.

Mum was experiencing similar nightly torments and she told me of one of her recurring dreams. Dad was marrying an extremely ugly woman in preference to my Mum. No-one present could understand why, least of all Mum. I thought that the woman represented cancer. It was cancer that had taken Dad away from her, an extremely ugly woman indeed and the dream left her feeling bereft.

Dreams were clearly a way of processing the experience and I remember one dream that was particularly healing. During the months leading up to Dad's death there was a complicated dynamic at work that made it impossible for me to honestly speak out the things that were on my mind. This was partly due to the denial that I spoke about earlier but also to the unwritten family rule of emotional repression. It may have been unwritten but it was as clear to me as if it had been written in neon lights across the sky. I felt its presence as it suffocated and silenced within me many of the words I wished to speak and so I never told Dad how I would miss him. It was in a dream that I was finally able to do this and I remember the warm glow of relief that was created by the utterance of those few simple words.

In another dream I was able to tell him that I loved him. In this dream he recovered: he didn't die. In my dream-world emotional honesty had saved him: in reality it brought me a sense of peace around his death.

We struggled through our waking life a day at a time each of us in our own way. My approach was to try to create a structure for my grief by investing in a beautiful, hard back notebook. It took me hours to choose it but it had to be just right in order to properly fulfil the enormous task it was intended for. I have always kept a journal. There is something I find extremely satisfying about the physical act of writing, of guiding my pen smoothly across paper. Chaotic thoughts assume structure; the vague becomes concrete and it gives me a sense of being in control.

My plan was for this carefully chosen notebook to be my grief journal. I planned to set time aside each week to give written expression to the shards of my grief and so move through to some kind of healing.

Being woefully short of rituals to guide us through grief, I decided to construct my own. So a pen was chosen with as much attention as the notebook had received and I prepared a table with the religious intensity of someone preparing a sacrificial altar. I lit a candle, burned essential oils and sat with pen poised above the blank pages of paper ready to give shape to the chaos of my grief and …...........................nothing!

I had not bargained on the maverick nature of grief which comes at a time of its own choosing and not mine. It hides round corners and lurks in the shadows biding its time, waiting for the chance to strike, always catching me unprepared, at times and in places where it might be least expected.

In the supermarket, for example, doing a weekly shop, my eyes fall on a box of Dad's favourite chocolate caramels. I used to buy him a box every Christmas along with his main present and it feels like I have been struck with a hammer blow as I realise I will never again buy my Dad those caramels.

Sometimes alone under the cloak of darkness I would cry and cry and cry out my loss until I feared I would never stop. How many tears are enough? I do not know. There is nowhere that tells me. This grief is something for which I'm totally unprepared. I have received no instruction or guidance for negotiating it so I simply have to make it up as I go along.

Some nights I am consumed with guilt when all my faults rise up to accuse me and all my past meannesses echo down the years; all the occasions when I was unkind or impatient with Dad or simply just took him for granted absorbed in my own life and concerns and not thinking too much about his; all the occasions, especially in his final days when I was physically present but emotionally absent. And I desperately wish for another chance to appreciate him more and just to be better.

At times my mind wanders without restraint through a labyrinth of thought and memories about my Dad when it is possible to believe that he is still around, that I could pick up the phone and hear his voice. But suddenly a door slams and I am faced with the indisputable hard fact that my Dad has gone FOR EVER, that I will never again see him in his physical form, never again share his corny jokes or receive his advice. He has cleaned my car for the very last time. He is no longer sorting tools and solving problems.

His absence is absolute, conclusive, decisive, definitive, incontrovertible, irrefutable, irrevocable, undeniable. He has gone, gone gone. I feel as though an enormous hole has opened up inside of me which it is impossible to fill. The physical sensation is similar to hunger or thirst that cannot be satisfied. So I feel as I might if I were starved of food or water, life's essentials. It is the finality that is so hard to bear and the sense of complete powerlessness to do anything to affect this hard, cold reality. In the face of death we are utterly powerless, a source of deep anger and frustration.

At times I think I see Dad living, breathing and walking along the pavement some way ahead of me. I quicken my pace to catch him but as I draw nearer I realise that I am mistaken. It isn't him, of course. I reluctantly remember it can't be him for he is dead and the dead don't walk the same pavements as the living.

My soaring spirits are immediately crushed with the recognition of this and I am consumed with a fiery and illogical anger that this stranger who had reminded me so much of my Dad is alive when he is not.

I have to police my response when friends speak of their fathers, careful not to betray the sharp teeth of resentment I feel for the continuance of their fathers when mine is no longer solid and dependable but reduced to ashes and blowing on the wind somewhere – who knows where.

When my Dad died everything changed for ever. As a result of his death I experience an increased sensitivity and discover that I have a capacity for sadness far deeper than I had ever imagined; a sadness always present just below the surface and ready to break through at the slightest disturbance. I feel forced to confront the meaning of my own life as I am confronted with my own mortality and I wonder what old age will be like for me and what I will leave behind. A part of me feels a sense of living for my Dad now as well as for myself and along with this comes a new responsibility to get the most out of life and live it to the full which is not quite as easy as the well worn phrases might suggest.

For a long time after his death I am haunted by images of his final suffering and struggle and it is only very gradually that he is restored to his former self. Finally he has his kindness and compassion back; his wit and sense of humour. He is almost totally restored to the strong, capable man of my early years; almost but not quite.

Although he has died, I gradually realise that I have not lost him. He is still available to me. Twenty three years have passed since his death and I still hear his voice as clearly as I ever did. In fact sometimes I think I hear him more clearly in death than I ever did in life when I was far more likely to skate over life's surface taking far too much for granted. Now it seems that there are many occasions when I know just exactly what he would say and what advice he might give. I can picture him clearly as I remember him now.

Grandma Brown as a young woman

Mum and Dad's Wedding
Standing: Grandpa Spendlove, Grandma Spendlove,
         Uncle Bill, My Dad, My Mum, Grandpa Brown
         Uncle Maurice, Uncle Jack
Seated: Grandma Brown, Aunt Margaret

The Spendlove family on holiday

Mum and Dad

Our beautiful cairn terrier, Bobby

Goodbye Mrs J

Death does not blow a trumpet.
Danish proverb

At the same time that we were struggling to come to terms with losing Dad, we were dealt a further crushing blow just a couple of weeks after Dad's funeral by a sudden and totally unexpected event.

One ordinary weekday morning Mrs Johnson, Mum's next door neighbour and close friend of many years, lurched awkwardly on her chair in her kitchen and took her final breath.

Mrs Johnson affectionately known as Mrs J was a significant figure in my childhood not in an intrusive way but more in the sense that she, like Dad, was always there. She would "pop round" via the short-cut that linked our two houses. She would suddenly appear at the back door, tap on one of its glass windows and wait to be let in. Her arrival was invariably signalled with the energy of a gale force wind.

Everything about Mrs J seemed large, not just her size. She appeared to have an inexhaustible supply of neighbourhood news and gossip. She had an enormous capacity for anxiety and concern not only for her own family but for ours too and she was prodigiously kind.

It was Mrs J, if you recall, who stepped in to feed and shelter me when as a young child I encountered my first experience of death. Her explanation at that time of my Aunt having, "gone to Jesus," stayed with me through the years and now Mrs J herself had "gone to Jesus". In stark contrast to my Dad who had endured a lingering death between the bed sheets, she died totally unexpectedly at the kitchen table while still seemingly engaged in the flow of life.

My Mum had just shared a cup of coffee and a chat with her and returned home when Mr J appeared at the glass window of her back door to seek her help with his wife. Together they followed the instructions of an anonymous voice at the end of a telephone line but in vain and when the paramedics finally arrived, she was pronounced dead. So not the slow slide from existence to non existence but more the here one minute, gone the next scenario of childhood imagining.

Mrs J was one of the ever present pillars of my childhood offering support and stability just by being there. It was as though I had constructed and internalised a paradigm of stability which when each part of it was in place and functioning appropriately all felt right with the world. Recent weeks had massively disturbed that paradigm and so severely shaken my sense of stability. All did definitely not feel right with the world. I had been administered a dose of impermanence almost too big to swallow and was struggling to know how to proceed.

Dad's death left little space in which to absorb the significance of this further loss but it stole odd moments whenever it could. Driving to work I would reflect on how things had changed so drastically and in such a short space of time. I realised that my sense of stability needed to be rooted less in externals and more within myself. This was a shift that was going to take time, a long time and is, in fact, a process that continues to this day. Part of this process is the acceptance of imperma- nence; the ability to live peacefully alongside the knowledge that all things pass. That is the nature of existence.

A Blessed Release

*What a simple thing death is, just as simple as
the falling of an autumn leaf.*
Vincent van Gogh

My Dad was just 72 when he died and it felt like he left
us too soon. It was clear from things that he said that
he himself did not feel quite ready to go. This was in
sharp contrast to my maternal Grandma who died some
years later. Gran lived to be 97 years old. She had
been born in 1900 and in those 97 years the world had
changed beyond recognition and by the time she
reached her old age she was tired, world weary and
ready to go.

Gran was a shy person, kept herself to herself and
didn't like a lot of fuss. She had not had an easy life.
She had lived through two world wars and was married
to a coal miner who had died young. Spending his days
in the bowels of the earth considerably shortened my
Grandpa's life. On one occasion he almost suffocated
when the roof of the pit collapsed on him pinning his
body beneath it. Although he survived this ordeal, it
inevitably took its toll on him and he suffered with lung
and heart complaints which gradually forced the life
from him leaving my Gran a widow in her fifities. So

she had learned to make the best of things, to grit her teeth and get on with life without complaint. She once had a broken wrist for days which she did not mention and which did not stop her from carrying on with her usual chores. She was tough was my Gran.

The last few years of her life had not been happy. She had been moved into a care home and she never really settled. Living in such close proximity to strangers did not suit her reserved character and such was the level of her dissatisfaction that she did uncharacteristically begin to complain.

She had outlived my Dad and during her time in the care home she outlived her own son, my Uncle Maurice, with whom she had been extremely close. Uncle Maurice had been suffering for some time with severe arthritis but his death from a heart attack was sudden and unexpected. Clearly someone had to break the tragic news to my Gran and Mum, anxious about the effect it would have on her, enlisted the support of myself and brother, Dave.

Gran's senses were severely blunted: her eyesight and hearing were fading making communication diffi-cult. And so when Mum first tried to break the news there was absolutely no reaction. Was this Gran's usual fortitude in the face of adversity? I wondered but it soon became clear that she had not understood. At that point I got the tiniest glimpse into how life was for my Gran. Surrounded by people and things she did not understand, no longer able to trust the evidence of her senses or rely on her body which had quite suddenly it seemed become unsteady and fragile, existence must

A Day I'll Never Forget

*The thing about hearts is that they always
want to keep beating.
Elizabeth Scott: "Living Dead Girl"*

Each time we experience death it reminds us of our own mortality and one day in 1999 I was even more powerfully confronted with that reality.

The day started just like any other. There was nothing to mark it as special in any way. At this time I was teaching at a school in Hertfordshire. As I recall it was the school Summer holiday. I think it was a Thursday. I had been into school to collect the GCSE results so it was early afternoon when I set off in my green Corsa up a very busy M1 to Derby.

The journey had been uneventful and I was travelling at about 80mph in the middle lane. I have a vague memory of a white transit van starting to pull into the lane in front of me but deciding against it and pulling back into the outside lane.

I was fast approaching my exit junction. My head began the thinking process behind the necessary manoeuvre when my eyes were taken with the reappearance of the white van. It was pulling in front of me after all and if I kept travelling at the speed I was I would smash into it.

I'm not totally sure what I did next. Whatever it was was purely a reflex response. Either I braked or swerved or did both at the same time. Whatever it was, it was the wrong thing the result being that I was swerving uncontrollably across all three lanes of the busy northbound carriageway of the M1.

I clutched tightly onto the steering wheel, my body rigid, once again instinctively doing all the wrong things. As I swung to the left I pulled down hard right on the wheel which sent me hurtling uncontrollably in the opposite direction. I kept repeating the process swerving recklessly from side to side, fighting with the wheel, desperate to right myself but the situation was not getting any better. If anything it was getting worse.

I clearly remember thinking, "Well I might as well give up". But then the thought sliced through me that this was literally a matter of life or death and giving up was therefore not an option. I was not ready to depart this world.

As the reality of the situation registered, I felt sheer unadulterated panic such as I had never felt before or since. It registered in my chest and in my stomach. My legs felt weak and the metallic taste of terror filled my mouth. For a few moments in which time seemed to stretch and slow, I was certain I was going to die. My life did not flash before my eyes as I had been lead to believe it would in such a situation. I wondered how my Mum would be informed and I had a flash of friends I did not want to leave.

Then everything went quiet. There was just me - inside my car – about to die and something in me relaxed – surrendered to my fate – a flash of the possibility that I may survive but be badly maimed. Surviving unharmed did not register as a possibility.

So I gave myself up to the inevitable as the central crash barrier loomed into view.

I hadn't given up, I had fought with the wheel for life right up to the inevitable conclusion. And here it was. I smashed head on into the barrier. The car spun round and was thrown back. There I was seated in my driving seat – still unharmed engulfed by an eerie silence. I was seated sideways across the centre lane of the motorway. The white van disappeared into the distance. Ahead of me were three deserted lanes and behind me three lines of traffic had stopped – stock still.

It took a moment or two for my head to catch up with the reality of what had happened. I sat totally still – stunned – unsure of what to do. I looked down at my legs which somehow seemed not to belong to me. There they were dressed in denim, solid and unharmed. The inside of the car was unchanged and the windscreen intact. External reality seemed undisturbed. It was all just as it had been before all this took place.

My mind seemed to be acting along tramlines of normality as the thought crossed it that I should not get out of my car in the middle lane of a motorway. But what had happened was far from normal. It seemed indeed that reality had slipped slightly and would never be quite the same again. I was imprinted with the realisation that everything can change in a heartbeat. I wasn't dead but I could so easily have been and my internal reality was forever altered.

After what seemed like a very long time, a stranger lead me out of the car to the safety of the hard shoulder. He was calm and kind though unable to tell me exactly what had happened for me as he had been locked in his own individual battle to avoid smashing into me.

My car was unceremoniously pushed out of the way as impatient motorists simply wanted to continue their journeys. Their normality was undisturbed – the wheels of life were turning once more.

Chris Cross and Wrong Cat Pat

Life does not cease to be funny when people die any more than it ceases to be serious when people laugh.
George Bernard Shaw

Chris Cross was a close friend of mine, the sort of friend I could drop in on just out of the blue. We cooked for each other and shared our problems and dissatisfactions as well as our triumphs and successes. Our conversations ranged over numerous subjects and I suppose you could say that we were easy in each other's company. He had had a major depression which had put him on the look-out for recurring symptoms, fearful in case the depression should return. Apart from that he seemed fairly healthy.

One Friday evening I was on my way home from work and suddenly remembered I had arranged to pop in on Chris. His house was on my homeward route but, by the time I remembered, I had gone way past it. Tired from a busy week, I did not feel like turning back so I cursed my forgetfulness and carried on.

As soon as I got home I rang Chris to explain my absence and give my apologies but I got no answer.

Chris was a guitar maker and was probably in his workshop out of earshot of the phone so I left a message and thought no more about it.

I heard nothing from Chris all day Saturday which I thought was a little odd but I fully expected to speak to him on Sunday. Every Sunday morning we attended a Tai Chi class with another friend, Mac, and it was our habit to contact each other to confirm our attendance before class but on Sunday I still had heard nothing from Chris. This was very out of character and left me feeling slightly uneasy and with a head full of questions. Had Chris gone away for a few days or was his phone out of order? Would he turn up to Tai Chi or did he have other plans?

Figuring that I would soon get an answer to these questions, I set off for class. On arrival I met Mac who also had heard nothing from Chris. When he had not shown up by the start of the class my feelings of unease intensified. Throughout the class all I could think about was what had happened to Chris. This no show with no explanation was so completely out of character but somehow I managed to convince myself that there would be a perfectly simple explanation. Nevertheless, I was hugely relieved when class finally came to an end and Mac and I decided to go round to Chris's to discover the solution to the mystery. Nothing could have prepared us for what we were to find.

It was a very hot, sunny day and when we arrived at Chris's house we noticed his windows were all open and the curtains were gently blowing in the breeze. So he hadn't gone away – very odd. Why then had he not been in touch in the usual way? First we checked his workshop but it was all locked up and he was not there. Next it was the house. Knocking on the door and getting no answer, our anxiety began to increase. Something here was very odd indeed. Things were not making sense. If he wasn't at home why would he leave all the windows wide open?

Our knocking became louder and more urgent until, peering through the open window, we caught sight of Chris's fractured legs sprawled across the floor. The situation looked extremely serious as Mac struggled in through the window then opened the door for me.

"He's gone!" said Mac quietly.

I was completely unable to take in the enormity of what was before me.

"What do you mean gone?" I demanded

"Gone," Mac repeated no doubt incredulous that I did not seem to be grasping what to him was patently obvious.

Chris was clearly unequivocally dead and we were the first to discover it.

The grim reality of the situation gradually permeated my resistance and it began to dawn on me that some action was needed although I was at a loss for what this might be. Here I was in a situation I had not encountered before and for which I was totally unprepared.

We knew we needed help and settled on calling the ambulance service even though it was obvious that Chris was way beyond any help they were likely to be able to give. Mac dialled the number and was almost immediately on the receiving end of instructions for

CPR. The phone operator was clearly working through routine procedure ignoring Mac's insistence that it was way too late for this. What an enormous relief it was when the paramedics finally arrived.

They needed us out of the way and swung into action with admirable efficiency. It was immediately obvious that they were used to functioning in such extreme circumstances and the scene exploded into busy activity as they confirmed what we already knew; namely that our friend had breathed his last and no amount of CPR was likely to change that. Phone-calls were made followed by the swift arrival of first the fire brigade and then the police.

Events took an unexpected and slightly alarming turn with the arrival of the police who told us to step outside and then designated the scene a crime scene informing us that we were not allowed to leave. Did they seriously believe that foul play was afoot and that we were implicated in it? Clearly they hadn't ruled it out and so we stood helplessly behind Chris's closed door as various strangers came and went and we struggled to take in what was happening.

The fire service had been called because there was a frying pan on the stove which was switched on, had heated the wall behind and had become dangerously close to bursting into flames. Had this been left much longer, we were informed, it was quite likely that the house would have gone up in flames and, given the fact that it was semi-detached, this would have had serious consequences for many more people. Thankfully it had been caught just in time.

I seem to recall using gallows' humour to lighten our situation until finally one of the police officers informed us that we should go. And so we did in something of a daze.

Arriving back at Mac's place, we realised that we needed to let people know what had happened and Mac made the particularly difficult call to Chris's brother who he charged with breaking the terrible news to his mother. Communicating such appalling news down the phone lines was devastating and we struggled to cope with other people's shock when we hadn't even begun to come to terms with our own.

Chris had died just out of the blue and the fact that he had a pan on the stove suggested that he was in the middle of cooking himself some food. It's quite likely that death and dying were the last things on his mind and I was reminded of the death of Mrs J which was equally sudden and unexpected although Chris was only 52 and Mrs J had been a great deal older.

It wasn't until this point that I began to wonder if we had done the right thing in walking away from Chris's house and leaving him in the hands of strangers although I felt that the policeman who suggested that we should leave was really issuing an instruction and no realistic alternative. Nevertheless, I was haunted by the guilt of these doubts.

Once again death had undermined my stability and, as I drew up at a roundabout on my drive home, I found myself completely unable to pull away. I was rooted to the spot, convinced that I was about to be killed by an oncoming vehicle. I was completely consumed by my sense of vulnerability, previous resilience totally forgotten and, although I finally managed to pull away and drive home, the sense that I could drop dead any minute persisted taking weeks to finally disappear and even then it left its trace.

The night of Chris's death three light bulbs exploded in my hallway; one that had been in a while and two new replacements. It reminded me of the car dials after my Dad's death and to this day I remain convinced that it was Chris's way of communicating with me and letting me know that he was okay.

Chris's death marked the beginning of a period of time that revolved completely around him. His family entrusted the planning of his funeral to his friends who they believed knew him best. I think they were right and it was an honour. On the day, however, despite meticulous planning, all did not go according to plan.

As I said before, Chris was a guitar maker, and a guy, who I did not know called Andy, had been chosen to perform using one of Chris's guitars. The service was held at Watford Crematorium and as the time drew close it began to be whispered around that Andy had not arrived. Crematoria have tight schedules and do not have the flexibility to delay the start time of any funeral. So as we filed inside there was a feeling of slight panic bubbling below the surface. The performance was an important part of the service. It was a tribute to Chris's guitar making skills and to who he was as a person. We didn't want Chris's family to regret handing over the service to his friends. The absence of a performance would feel like we had let

Chris down, that we had failed to give him the send off that he deserved. And so the service began.

Andy did not show up until the service was well over and, since it was in the days before mobile phones were commonplace, he was unable to let people know the situation. It was, therefore, at the very last moment that another friend, Pete, picked up one of Chris's guitars, gave a short verbal introduction and performed "*Stand By Me*". It was unrehearsed and touching and it somehow reached beneath the surface of things and represented something real about who Chris was. It made me smile because Chris hated that song but he would have found the incident and final irony amusing and he would have loved the spirit in which Pete had stepped in and offered up a heartfelt and genuine tribute to the friend he had lost.

Much later it was discovered that Andy's car had got locked in a car park and, despite his best efforts, he had been unable to free it before the service was over. As it happened, it hadn't spoilt the funeral but I bet it has remained a source of regret for Andy. If death itself had not been enough to illustrate that we are not in as much control as we like to think we are, then surely what happened to Andy would be enough to convince us.

There was a fair amount of chaos around Chris's passing clearly illustrated not only by events at the funeral but also by another incident which definitely had its funny side.

Once Chris's family had been notified of his death, his brother and sister-in-law made their way up to

St Albans to sort things out. Sudden death leaves so much to be done. At a time when we feel most vulnerable and least efficient we are called upon to attend to a complex set of practicalities and Chris's brother was struggling to clear up the mess Chris had left behind including a daunting pile of paperwork. In the midst of all this he had encountered Chris's cat who we worked out must have been with Chris's lifeless body for a couple of days. How much understanding do animals have of death? I have no idea. They experience the world through instinct and I was not surprised that the cat was in a state of distress. He was clearly traumatised and presented one problem too many for Chris's brother who asked if we would sort him out, a task that proved to be way more difficult than we imagined.

Once we had found someone willing to have the cat we considered the mission to be more or less completed. How wrong we were. The creature was so traumatised that he wouldn't allow anyone to get even close. Numerous people tried numerous strategies to ensnare him but on every occasion the humans were outwitted. We were beginning to despair when Pat, a close friend of Chris's, announced that her son was particularly good with animals and would more than likely be able to persuade Chris's cat into being captured.

The next we heard, Pat's son had been successful. The cat had apparently put up little resistance and was comfortably installed in his new home. Job done! What a relief! We delivered the news to Chris's brother and turned our attention to other matters.

A couple of days later, however, Mac answered his phone to the voice of Chris's confused brother saying, "I thought you had sorted out the cat!" Mac replied confidently that we had, only to hear that he had reappeared at Chris's house. Further investigation revealed that the cat that Pat's son had so effortlessly captured and rehomed was not Chris's cat at all but an innocent bystander who happened to get caught up in all the confusion. He had been catnapped and relocated and he was somebody else's cat. That somebody else would doubtless be missing their moggy.

And so it was that under cover of darkness the unwitting catnappers stole out to release their conquest back into the freedom of the night. No wonder Pat's son had secured the cat so easily and it had nothing to do with his Dr Dolittle credentials.

The tale has a satisfactory resolution as we finally used a very large portion of the very best salmon to lure the right cat into captivity and transport him to his new home. It took a while for him to calm down and readjust but he gradually managed it. And ever afterwards Mac and I always referred to Pat as Wrong Cat Pat although I don't think she ever knew this.

Mum's Death

When we lose one we love, our bitterest tears are
called forth by the memory of hours when
we loved not enough.
Maurice Maeterlinck: "Wisdom and Destiny"

Mum died in June 2008, fourteen years after Dad. During that time she was able to construct a life without him that she was able to enjoy. I know she missed him terribly after spending most of her adult life with him and for the first couple of years after his death she forced herself to do things she would rather not, preferring to stay at home or to be with the family. Gradually, however, she developed a solid group of friends with who she shared various activities and seemed to be fairly happy. I'm not sure we would have known had she not been. She was very skilled at masking negative feelings and suppressing them in the old family way. On reflection, I think this may have been a coping mechanism for many of Mum's generation who had lived through the atrocities of war and been taught the art of the "stiff upper lip".

Sadly, however, Mum did have health issues in the form of scleroderma, a degenerative disorder which slowly but surely made its vicious attack.

Mum's death for me was more complex than Dad's somehow, partly because her illness spanned so many years and partly also because of the nature of my relationship with her. Perhaps it is for these reasons that I find myself reluctant to relive those years and yet to omit the experience of Mum's death in a memoir such as this would be a glaring and inexplicable omission. My compromise is to treat it here with brevity with the possibility of returning to it at some future time.

As Mum's illness made its deadly advance it created symptoms which became steadily more and more dramatic culminating in the amputation of her right leg. It seemed more like something from the Crimean War than twenty first century Britain – primitive and brutal and I could not begin to imagine what it might have been like for Mum. I find it almost impossible to convey how deeply this affected me.

Up to this point my brother, Dave, had been Mum's main carer and so he would remain. He and I accompanied each other as Mum underwent the amputation and no doubt his account of events would be very different to mine. That is his to tell.

For my part, I desperately sought the reassurance of the medical professionals and tried to cope with it by not allowing myself to think too much about the gruesome reality of the situation. My focus was on staying positive to support Mum through the operation and both Dave and I kept our minds off it by shopping for the various things Mum would need for her prolonged hospital stay. My concern that she might not make it through remained largely unspoken and in the end Mum was subjected to three such operations on three separate occasions, each one higher up the leg, before it was deemed to have been successful. This certainly took an emotional toll on us all. By the third one Mum herself seriously doubted her ability to survive. But she did.

And she faced all this with fortitude and real spirit. She put all her energy into adapting to life with only one leg refusing to be beaten but her mobility was seriously restricted and over time the parameters of her life shrank until much of it was confined to the house, her only view of the outside world being through the window. She did, however, have a gift for finding pleasure in simple things – a robin in the garden, the first spring flowers, a fox cub on the lawn and so much more. The young country girl inside her loved the changing seasons and for some years she managed to sustain some joy in life and some interest in all that was going on around her.

Some years ago I worked in a school for young people described as having "severe learning difficulties". In reality they all had their own challenging health issues which made ordinary life extremely difficult for them. These children came into school every day often with smiles on their faces and a spring in their steps ready and willing to have a go at whatever might be asked of them, often failing to achieve what they had set out to do but never being defeated by it and knowing that the following day they would try again with equal enthusiasm and determination to succeed. These people to me are the heroes of modern life and my Mum joined these ranks after her amputation. She just got on with life, embracing the struggle and with little complaint.

Scleroderma does not stand still, however, and over a number of years Mum's condition noticeably deteriorated. I moved back to the Midlands to support Dave with Mum's care and found this extremely stressful. I had to adapt to a new house, a new job which I hated and a new location. Although it had been my childhood home, it had changed beyond recognition since those days. I had left my friends and hence my support network back in Hertfordshire and was not able to support Mum as much as she clearly expected.

By this time she appeared to have lost the ability to appreciate the needs of other family members and, while Dave remained the main carer, I began to feel that however often I visited and whatever I might do, it would never be enough. And always at the back of all our minds I think was the unvoiced anxiety that although things were bad they could still get worse and if they did how would we all cope?

Mum was now on so much medication that she frequently experienced drug psychosis which put her in a completely different reality to the one the rest of us were inhabiting. Sometimes this seemed amusing but at other times it was extremely disturbing. At one point she confided in a visiting friend that she believed we were keeping her prisoner against her will and she tried to persuade this friend to assist her in her bid for freedom. I guess aspects of her existence were rather similar to imprisonment. Often she was convinced that she was surrounded by malevolence in some form or other, sometimes people who were deliberately taunting her at other times worm-like creatures on which she waged war cutting through cloth and scraping through wood in order to vanquish them.

At times she would be unpleasantly hostile, not like her real self at all and it began to seem as though my Mum had virtually disappeared. Although there were times of lucidity, the Mum who had looked after and cared for other people for most of her life appeared less and less frequently. Her life had become just pain and struggle no longer offset by the simple pleasures and this was unbearably hard to witness.

So when death came it brought along with the grief a strong sense of relief. The suffering which had gone on for so long was finally over and I would no longer have to worry about how much worse things might get. However, this was only part of the experience.

Out of the shadows stepped Guilt with its relentless taunting, parading before me the numerous occasions when I had fallen short in caring for my Mum, when I had been impatient or neglectful, wrapped up in my own concerns while she was battling with issues way more serious than mine.

It took some time to get beyond those images and to recall my Mum as she used to be and, although we did not always see eye to eye, I missed that person unequivocally and I still do. I never doubted that she wanted the best for me even while we may not always have agreed what that might be. We inhabited very different worlds but she was always in my corner and totally loyal. There are few people in life so dependable. I would often catch myself planning to call Mum when for a split second I believed her to be still alive – still do, in fact, over 11 years later and I carry her with me just as I do Dad.

I found losing a second parent significantly different to losing the first, not only because it is a different relationship that is lost but also because it seems that there is no longer anyone standing between me and the grave. I feel a strong sense of my own fragility and ultimately my own mortality; a sense both frightening and profound; a sense that throws up those existential questions regarding the meaning of existence and non existence, of life and death. The seeds of my search for meaning were planted in childhood, if not before, and that search has continued throughout my life and continues still.

Death Becomes
More Frequent

Dust thou art and unto dust shalt thou return
"Genesis 3:19"

As I get older, deaths of people I know or have known have become more frequent.

I recall sitting in a hospice with a friend as he died. It seemed quite peaceful as I watched him take his final breath and it made me sad because, although he had been an old friend, our lives had progressed in different directions and we had seen little of each other in later years. Accompanying someone to the threshold of death is a privilege. It is a profoundly moving and intimate experience but I would have liked my old friend to have walked that path with someone he was closer to. I wonder why I feel that matters. I believe that people often die alone and that this is their choice, that it is easier to loosen the grip on life when there is no-one close by struggling to keep them earthbound.

In that final vigil with my friend I strived to be fully present, wrestling the wayward nature of my mind which constantly fought to smash through the confines of that small room in whatever flights of fancy might serve to make the ordeal itself less intense, more easily bearable. Was it Elliot who said, "Mankind cannot stand too much reality"?

In sharp contrast to this experience, I remember hearing third hand and months after the event that my Uncle Jack had died. Uncle Jack had played a significant role in my life at various times most especially in childhood and also around the time of my Dad's death. Mum's protracted illness had absorbed much of my attention and I felt I had little left over for anyone else which meant that regular communication with other family members fell away. I was aware that Uncle Jack was struggling after the death of his wife my Aunt Margaret but I felt unable to help and so shut out the extent of his suffering; something I will always regret. It never occurred to me that he might depart this life without my knowing. It was my understanding that when a family member died there would, at the very least, be a phone-call to let relatives know. That's how it had always been and there was no reason to think that had changed.

But it had! And I was appalled to discover months later that not only had Uncle Jack died but his funeral had taken place and his body reduced to ashes and all without my knowledge. I had not had the opportunity to say goodbye or to pay my respects. How could that have happened?

I guess death had been gradually dismantling the family network that ensured the communication of such important news. I had somehow assumed that my parents would always be there to perform the role they played in this and I had failed to revisit this assumption in the wake of their deaths. It took the death of Uncle Jack for me to realise that the channel of family communication which had been there all my life had been shut down with the departure of my parents.

A relative whose death I did hear about was my Auntie Edna. She wasn't really my auntie, she was my Mum's cousin but that's what we called her. Auntie Edna was another significant figure in my childhood and as a child I used to think of her as elegant and exciting. I was struggling with the basics of learning to play the piano and whenever Auntie Edna arrived at our house, it would come alive as her fingers danced over the ivories to produce some of the most exquisite music. I was filled with admiration and desperate to be able to emulate her in this respect.

Auntie Edna suffered over many years with Alzheimers Disease and took her leave very gradually. Her music was silenced well before she died and it was no surprise to receive the phone-call reporting her death. For her daughters who watched her suffer and bore the full burden of her illness, it may have been in some ways a relief but even though it had been creeping up little by little over the years when death finally came I still felt terribly sad and I'm quite sure they did too.

By way of contrast the death of my long time friend Michael seemed to come almost out of the blue just as Chris's had. It was a very ordinary day and we had been walking in the Peak District enjoying the fresh air and exercise. On returning home we received a phone-call to say that Michael had died suddenly and unexpectedly. I found it almost impossible to grasp what I was being told. Although he had experienced some health issues in recent years, there was never any suggestion that they were life threatening or if they were I had been in denial. Is it true that we fail to see what we would rather not? I'm sure that at times it is.

Michael had been a close friend for over forty years and it seemed unbelievable that he could just check out like this with little apparent warning. Experience had already taught me that this could indeed happen but it was a lesson I clearly had to learn again and, while I know it to be true that life can be snatched away with little apparent warning, it seems impossible to live fully in that knowledge.

As time passes it is more and more punctuated by the occurrence of death and I have not included all those I have lost in these pages. While death becomes more frequent it is never commonplace. I register the enormity of every passing and am struck very differently by each one. No two deaths are the same either in themselves or in their significance for me.

Final Reflections

Let us endeavour so to live that when we come to
die even the undertaker will be sorry.
Mark Twain:"Pudd'nhead Wilson"

For all my encounters with death, I have come no closer to unlocking its mysteries and inevitably it continues to weave itself into the fabric of my existence.

One evening I sat watching with half an eye a television programme called *"The Repair Shop"*. In the programme people bring broken objects with great sentimental value to a team of craftsmen to be repaired. My attention was suddenly caught by the appearance of a dilapidated teddy bear. This bear had certainly lived. It was missing an ear, had no eyes or nose and, in fact, hardly resembled a bear at all.

A young woman was telling its story and it slowly began to dawn on me that this bear had belonged to someone I had known years ago, a friend of my brother called Ian. Further details and a photograph of him confirmed my suspicions. This teddy had belonged to Ian and had made its way to *"The Repair Shop"* because he had recently died very suddenly with little time to say goodbye and his family felt that restoring the treasured teddy to its former glory before life took its inevitable toll would be a fitting tribute to Ian. This was certainly something they couldn't do for Ian himself.

The story was deeply touching and lead me to trawl back through the box of old family photographs until I found one of sports day at Cherry Tree Hill Junior School. There was the red team and there on the back row was Ian – ten years old, full of life and eyes alight with anticipation of the day and possibly of all the rest of the unknown that lay before him. There is something profoundly moving about a little boy frozen in time, smiling down the years beyond his own death to a teddy that has survived the wear and tear of life (just!) to outlive him.

Was it Beckett who pointed out that we are born astride the grave? Certainly I do feel that we are born with the seeds of our mortality and I continue to be captivated by this just as I was as a child. I am still drawn to graveyards in the same way that I was drawn to Ann Brontë's grave all those years ago. They have a magnetic pull that I find hard to resist. People may seek to establish supremacy through deliberately ostentatious memorials but it's a hollow gesture as there is no escaping the fact that death is the great leveller. At the end of life we are all finally returned to the earth where there is no hierarchy of worth. Graveyards are real places in which we are stripped of everything.

There is a cemetery very close to where I now live. It is calm, serene, a quiet place I go to for reflection; to sit on one of its benches, to walk along its deserted paths, to observe the changing seasons and just to be. At times there is a beautiful, watery, Autumn sun highlighting the magnificent colours of the falling leaves: headstones set out in rows of almost military precision; ordered, contained.

Some are simple with the barest of inscriptions,

Alice Farley

1908 – 1991

RIP

while others bear elaborate illustrations in an attempt to distil the essence of the departed: a boat for a sailor, spade and flowers for a gardener, the face of a much loved dog. Many of the inscriptions favour rhyme and speak in language which makes the departure seem ordinary, "called home", "fell asleep", "at rest at last" - efforts to contain and to name this most solemn of mysteries.

Graves are strewn with a myriad different tokens: photographs, candles, plants and, perhaps most poignant of all, so called everlasting flowers beautifully crafted from silk and satin but unfortunately named for everything in this place bears witness to the harsh, stone fact that nothing lasts for ever.

I am drawn to individual graves whose inscriptions generate narratives. "So sorry we never got chance to resolve our differences,"says a mother to the body of her 32 year old son. "You left one morning. We didn't know you would never return. No chance to say goodbye," lament the family of a 59 year old woman.

There are the recent graves of six children from the same family who all died on the same day. I remember the tragedy and the outpouring of grief on the day that wiped out that whole family of children. How many tears are enough for the deaths of all these children? Here there are just simple wooden crosses to bear witness to their short lives.

Beyond these graves is the baby garden separated with a wrought iron archway. Here the tiny graves are alive with all the newborns might have owned: windmills spinning furiously in the wind, lanterns, ink smudged cards, teddies, fairies, plastic trucks, a plastic saxophone - toys they never got to hold. For these children were "born asleep" their bodies buried in the cold earth before they got chance to draw breath.

At Christmas time the place seems to throb with the colours of Christmas. Individual graves are adorned with holly wreaths, the flaming colours of poinsettias, shiny baubles, a whisky glass of Christmas roses. If it's Christmas anywhere, it's certainly Christmas here. Perhaps when the gates close the spirits rise and dance out the year, celebrating under the moonlight.

At the furthest corner of the cemetery are the graves of those long forgotten; overgrown, neglected; inscriptions faded and obscured with moss and lichen; ivy thrusting its tentacles around the crumbling stone of angels with broken wings. To the south is a flat, grassed field – empty and waiting to receive the bodies of those still living.

It feels as if the whole of existence is here in this graveyard and yet it remains a quiet place, a place of reflection.

It seems paradoxical to say that death gives life meaning but I know it to be true. I remember reading

Swift's account of the Struldbrugs who were given the gift of everlasting life. It soon became clear that the gift was a poisoned chalice as they deteriorated to a state from which death would have served as a blessed release. Clearly for Swift immortality was not desirable and yet perhaps there is a small part of all of us that yearns for it nonetheless.

I find myself wishing that a slight imprint of my footfall may endure after the foot itself has departed; that I may breathe a little longer through other lives I may have touched; that my voice somehow might whisper down the years long after I am gone.

But maybe part of life's purpose is the gradual acceptance of mortality of our own and of everyone around us. Nothing is for ever. Life is change just as the seasons change and so we must adapt and let go.

Every death I have experienced has made its imprint on me and provoked a shifting of my inner landscape. The shift might have been subtle or it might have been seismic but every one has helped to shape who I now am. I know that death will continue to walk alongside me and will ultimately take me to whatever does or does not exist beyond it.

Afterword

I thought that I had completed my final chapter and placed my final full stop but death does not work like that. It smashes with ease through any boundaries that I might choose to erect and, as it turns out, I was sleepwalking into something resembling a nightmare with no end in sight.

If I have learnt anything about death over the years it is that it appears in many different guises. I have heard it said that on some level we choose the time and manner of our own passing and, while this may at times be true, it is not always how it has seemed to me. Death, like grief, often seems to come in the form it wishes and at a time of its own choosing. It is the great disrupter and can strike when it's least expected. It has the capacity to shock us to our very core. I bear witness to this fact even now as I write for the nightmare that I have unwittingly stumbled into is a chaotic world with death at its centre. Death has stepped out of the shadows to occupy the full glare of centre stage.

Had I been more alert I might have seen it coming. It had its beginning in China and I was only dimly aware of it as it was reported on the evening news. It seemed so geographically distant that I did not seriously consider that it might have anything much to do with me. Even when it advanced its progress into Europe I naively failed to pay it much attention. After all there had been a lot of speculation in the past relating to the possibility of swine flu, avian flu and SARS engulfing us and all the warnings had come to nothing so why should this be any different?

But it is and it seems as though almost overnight normality has forever changed. The words Covid 19 are repeated countless times every day as the news exclusively reports the progress of this global pandemic. The rising death toll is updated daily passing the projected twenty thousand with alarming speed and now already more than double that. It seems that death has become an insatiable beast indiscriminately devouring all in its path.

In order to limit the spread of infection and to tame this beast, we are told to stay at home, wear masks, use hand sanitiser, frequently wash hands. Socially distancing, self isolating and shielding have become the normal modes of existence. Almost everything has closed down . Life has changed beyond all recognition as we are forced to confront death on such a massive scale.

Not personally knowing anybody so far who has suffered from Covid 19 creates a strange sense of unreality about it all. It feels as if we are existing in a bubble remote from all that is going on beyond it. Then television images of intensive care units temporarily penetrate the bubble; images that convey the shocking reality of what is happening and which continue to haunt me long after they have faded from the screen. It is the human face of the daily statistics: medics striving to save the lives of ordinary people engaged in a battle they don't always win. And for every person who dies many more are profoundly affected by the loss. We are confronted with our own fragility on a daily basis, knowing that none of us is safe.

I have no idea how the situation will continue to unfold. No-one can predict it although many are trying. Much that we have taken for granted has been swept away and life's essential uncertainty is laid bare.

We are walking unknown paths unsure of our destination and it remains to be seen how successfully we negotiate our way through. We have much to reflect on in order to learn the lessons this pandemic might be teaching us.

When the earth shall claim your limbs, then shall you truly dance.
Kahlil Gibran: "The Prophet"

Lightning Source UK Ltd.
Milton Keynes UK
UKHW011855301120
374392UK00001B/62